JESSICA BARRERA • Sallie Tomato

Essential Bag Making
REFERENCE TOOL

Complete Guide to Materials,
Bag Styles & Techniques

TIPS & TROUBLESHOOTING SOLUTIONS

Text and photography copyright © 2025 by Jessica Barrera

Artwork copyright © 2025 by C&T Publishing, Inc.

Publisher: Amy Barrett-Daffin

Creative Director: Gailen Runge

Senior Editor: Roxane Cerda

Editors: Madison Moore, Liz Aneloski

Technical Editors: Helen Frost, Debbie Rodgers

Cover/Book Designer: April Mostek

Production Coordinator: Zinnia Heinzmann

Illustrator: Mary E. Flynn

Photography Coordinators: Rachel Ackley, Lauren Herberg

Front cover photography by Jessica Barrera

Photography by Jessica Barrera, unless otherwise noted

Published by C&T Publishing, Inc., P.O. Box 1456, Lafayette, CA 94549

All rights reserved. No part of this work covered by the copyright hereon may be used in any form or reproduced by any means—graphic, electronic, or mechanical, including photocopying, recording, taping, or information storage and retrieval systems—without written permission from the publisher. The copyrights on individual artworks are retained by the artists as noted in *Essential Bag Making Reference Tool*. These designs may be used to make items for personal use only and may not be used for the purpose of personal profit. Items created to benefit nonprofit groups, or that will be publicly displayed, must be conspicuously labeled with the following credit: "Designs copyright © 2025 by Jessica Barerra from the book *Essential Bag Making Reference Tool* from

C&T Publishing, Inc." Permission for all other purposes must be requested in writing from C&T Publishing, Inc.

Attention Teachers: C&T Publishing, Inc., encourages the use of our books as texts for teaching. You can find lesson plans for many of our titles at ctpub.com or contact us at ctinfo@ctpub.com.

We take great care to ensure that the information included in our products is accurate and presented in good faith, but no warranty is provided, nor are results guaranteed. Having no control over the choices of materials or procedures used, neither the author nor C&T Publishing, Inc., shall have any liability to any person or entity with respect to any loss or damage caused directly or indirectly by the information contained in this book. For your convenience, we post an up-to-date listing of corrections on our website (ctpub.com). If a correction is not already noted, please contact our customer service department at ctinfo@ctpub.com or P.O. Box 1456, Lafayette, CA 94549.

Trademark (™) and registered trademark (®) names are used throughout this book. Rather than use the symbols with every occurrence of a trademark or registered trademark name, we are using the names only in the editorial fashion and to the benefit of the owner, with no intention of infringement.

Library of Congress Control Number: 2025936850

Printed in China

10 9 8 7 6 5 4 3 2 1

Dedication

To my mom—from the very first stitches to the biggest moments of my life, thank you for being there for me and encouraging me to follow my dreams. Not only did you teach me how to sew, but also how to problem-solve, have patience, and embrace challenges.

This book is a reflection of everything you've instilled in me, and I hope it inspires others the way you have always inspired me.

Acknowledgments

A heartfelt thank you to my husband, mom, brother, mother-in-law, and friends for all of your support and encouragement. Thank you to the thoughtful team at C&T Publishing for your enthusiasm, attention to detail, and guidance. I'm truly grateful to be asked to author this book.

Also, a special thank you to my incredible Sallie Tomato team—your dedication, creativity, and passion for bag making inspire me every day. Thank you for bringing our shared vision to life, for believing in the beauty of handcrafted bags, and for making this journey so fulfilling.

Contents

Introduction 6

Quick Reference Guides 7

Part 1
All About Bags 11

Types of Bags & Bag Composition 11
- Parts of a Bag 11
- Accordion Bags 12
- Backpacks, Daypacks & Rucksacks 12
- Baguette 13
- Barrel Bags 13
- Bowling Bags 13
- Bracelet & Wristlet Bags 14
- Bucket Bags 14
- Camera Bags 14
- Canteen Bags 15
- Clutches 15
- Crossbody & Sling Bags 15
- Diaper Bags 16
- Doctor's Bags 16
- Dopp Kits & Cosmetic Bags .. 16
- Drawstring Bags 17
- Duffle Bags 17
- Handbags 17
- Hobo Bags 18
- Insulated Bags 18
- Laptop, Briefcase & Portfolio Bags 18
- Messenger Bags 19
- Packing Cubes 19
- Pouches 19
- Saddle Bags 20
- Shoulder Bags 20
- Specialty Bags 20
- Tote Bags 21
- Waist Bags 21

Bag Care 22
- Cleaning & Conditioning 22
- Organizing & Care Accessories 23
- Top 10 Tips 24

Part 2
Making Bags 25

Fabrics & Interfacing 25
- Fabrics 25
  - Canvas 26
  - Cork 26
  - Cotton 27
  - Denim 27
  - Essex Linen 28
  - Faux Leather 28
  - Flannel 29
  - Fur & Faux Fur 29
  - Kraft-tex 30
  - Laminated Cotton 30
  - Leather 30
  - Mesh 31
  - Oilcloth 31
  - Sequins 32
  - Suede & Microsuede 32
  - Ripstop 33
  - Velvet & Velveteen 33
  - Vinyl 34
  - Waxed Canvas 34
- Interfacing & Support Materials 35
  - What Is Interfacing? 35

  Types & Best Uses of
  Interfacing 35
  Types & Best Uses of Support
  Materials 38
Hardware 40
 Bag Feet 41
 Buckles 42
 Chain 44
 Conchos 44
 Cord Locks 44
 Frames 45
 Grommets & Eyelets 46
 Key Fobs 46
 Labels 46
 Locks & Closures 47
 Magnetic Snaps 50
 Metal Handles 51
 Rings 51
 Rivets & Chicago Screws 54
 Snap Fasteners 54
 Spots 56
 Strap Arches 56
 Strap Connectors 56
 Strap Ends 56
 Stud Buttons 57
 Swivel Hooks 57
 Tassel Caps 58
 Zipper & Cord Ends 58
Handbag Zippers 59
 Anatomy of a Zipper 60
 Sizes 60
 Teeth 60
 Zipper Types & Applications .. 62
  Closed-End 62
  Separating 62
  Double-Slide Zippers 62
  Invisible 63
  Zipper by the Yard 64

Tools & Notions for Bag
Making 64
 Thread 65
 Needles 65
 Presser Feet 67
 Marking Tools 71
 Adhesives 72
 Pressing Tools 73
 Cutting Tools 74
 Hardware Tools 75
 Other Handy Items 78

Part 3
Bag Making Skills 81
Structure & Shaping 81
 Interfacing, Stabilizing &
 Reducing Bulk 82
 Adding Depth & Shape 83
  Boxed Bottom 83
  Darts 84
  Gussets 85
  Sewing Curves 85
Closures, Pockets, Straps &
Handles 86
 Closures 86
  Drawstring 86
  Magnetic Snap 87
  Purse Frame 87
  Top Zipper 88
 Essential Pockets 89
  Slip Pocket 89
  Zipper Pocket 90
 Straps & Handles 92
  Adjustable Strap 92
  Basic Shoulder Strap &
  Handles 93
  Wristlet Strap 94

Index 95
About the Author 96

Introduction

Bag making is a journey—one filled with creativity, problem-solving, and the excitement of transforming simple materials into something both beautiful and functional. Whether you're stitching your very first bag or refining your skills, this reference tool is here to guide you every step of the way.

Like many sewists, I once found myself wondering why handmade bags didn't always have the same polished, professional look as store-bought ones. I knew there had to be a secret—a formula for success. Through years of experimenting, learning, and teaching others, I cracked the code. Now, I want to share that knowledge with you.

This compact yet comprehensive guide is designed to be your go-to resource for everything bag making—materials, hardware, construction techniques, troubleshooting tips, and more. Bags are endlessly customizable, and with the right knowledge, the possibilities become exciting rather than overwhelming.

No matter where you are in your sewing journey, I hope this book empowers you to create confidently. Keep it in your sewing space, flip through it when you need guidance, and most importantly—have fun. Your next favorite bag is just a few stitches away!

Quick Reference Guides

This book is a treasure trove of knowledge! Browsing through will surely give you inspiration and resources for your next bag project. But, if you already know what you're looking for, you might want to use a quick reference guide in this chapter to jump around.

 You're a Beginner...

BAG TYPES
- Drawstring Bags (page 17)
- Pouches (page 19)
- Tote Bags (page 21)

SUGGESTED MATERIALS
- Cork (page 26)
- Canvas (page 26)
- Cotton (page 27)

SUGGESTED HARDWARE
- Handbag Zippers (page 59)
- Rings (page 51)

KEY SKILLS REFERENCE
- Closures (page 86)
- Essential Pockets (page 89)

 You Want to Work with Leather...

BAG TYPES
- Dopp Kits & Cosmetic Bags (page 16)
- Saddle Bag (page 20)
- Crossbody & Sling Bags (page 15)
- Canteen Bags (page 15)

SUGGESTED MATERIALS & TOOLS
- Faux Leather (page 28)
- Leather (page 30)
- Leather Needle (page 65)
- Roller Foot (page 69)
- Teflon Foot (page 70)

SUGGESTED HARDWARE
- Bag Feet (page 41)
- Slider (page 43)
- Chain (page 44)
- Grommets & Eyelets (page 46)
- Tassel Caps (page 58)
- Hammers & Mallets (page 75)

KEY SKILLS REFERENCE
- Straps and Handles (page 92)
- Bag Care (page 22)
- Adhesives (page 72)

You're Going Out on the Town...

BAG TYPES
- Bracelet & Wristlet Bags (page 14)
- Clutches (page 15)
- Waist Bags (page 21)
- Crossbody & Sling Bags (page 15)

SUGGESTED MATERIALS
- Sequins (page 32)
- Fur & Faux Fur (page 29)
- Faux Leather (page 28)
- Leather (page 30)
- Suede & Microsuede (page 32)
- Velvet & Velveteen (page 33)

SUGGESTED HARDWARE
- Chain (page 44)
- Conchos (page 44)
- Locks & Closures (page 47)
- Metal Handles (page 51)
- Strap Connectors (page 56)
- Tassel Caps (page 58)

KEY SKILLS REFERENCE
- Adding Depth & Shape (page 83)
- Zipper Pocket (page 90)
- Purse Frame (page 87)

 You Want a Quilted Bag...

BAG TYPES
- Tote Bags (page 21)
- Pouches (page 19)
- Drawstring Bags (page 17)
- Insulated Bags (page 18)

SUGGESTED MATERIALS & TOOLS
- Cotton (page 27)
- Essex Linen (page 28)
- Flannel (page 29)
- Velvet & Velveteen (page 33)
- Walking Foot (page 70)
- Marking Tools (page 71)
- Bias Tape (page 78)

SUGGESTED HARDWARE
- Buckles (page 42)
- Rings (page 51)
- Handbag Zippers (page 59)

KEY SKILLS REFERENCE
- Drawstring (page 86)
- Top Zipper (page 88)
- Adjustable Strap (page 92)

You Need a Roomy Bag...

BAG TYPES
- Duffle Bags (page 17)
- Backpacks, Daypacks & Rucksacks (page 12)
- Diaper Bags (page 16)
- Doctor's Bags (page 16)

SUGGESTED MATERIALS
- Canvas (page 26)
- Cotton (page 27)
- Denim (page 27)
- Essex Linen (page 28)
- Waxed Canvas (page 34)
- Mesh (page 31)

SUGGESTED HARDWARE
- Rings (page 51)
- Strap Arches (page 56)
- Strap Connectors (page 56)
- Swivel Hooks (page 57)
- Buckles (page 42)

KEY SKILLS REFERENCE
- Top Zipper (page 88)
- Adjustable Strap (page 92)
- Slip Pocket (page 89)
- Zipper Pocket (page 90)

You're Heading to the Farmer's Market...

BAG TYPES
- Insulated Bags (page 18)
- Tote Bags (page 21)
- Waist Bags (page 21)
- Backpacks, Daypacks & Rucksacks (page 12)

SUGGESTED MATERIALS
- Canvas (page 26)
- Cotton (page 27)
- Laminated Cotton (page 30)
- Oilcloth (page 31)

SUGGESTED HARDWARE
- Key Fobs (page 46)
- Buckles (page 42)
- Rings (page 51)

KEY SKILLS REFERENCE
- Adjustable Strap (page 92)
- Zipper Pocket (page 90)
- Drawstring (page 86)
- Top Zipper (page 88)
- Basic Shoulder Straps & Handle (page 93)

QUICK REFERENCE GUIDES

You Need a Bag Inside Another Bag...

BAG TYPES

- Packing Cubes (page 19)
- Pouches (page 19)
- Dopp Kits & Cosmetic Bags (page 16)

SUGGESTED MATERIALS

- Kraft-tex (page 30)
- Canvas (page 26)
- Laminated Cotton (page 30)
- Oilcloth (page 31)
- Velvet & Velveteen (page 33)
- Vinyl (page 34)

SUGGESTED HARDWARE

- Grommets & Eyelets (page 46)
- Locks & Closures (page 47)
- Magnetic Snaps (page 50)
- Snap Fasteners (page 54)

KEY SKILLS REFERENCE

- Top Zipper (page 88)
- Drawstring (page 86)
- Slip Pocket (page 89)
- Wristlet Strap (page 94)

PART ONE
All About Bags

TYPES OF BAGS & BAG COMPOSITION

Throughout history, bags have evolved according to the needs of the times. Some designs have been maintained over centuries, carrying through into the present day, and new types of bags have developed. Every day we use bags to simplify how we carry various items. There are so many varieties of each type of bag; however, there are usually a few key features that define it. A bag's name is often derived from its form, its purpose, how it's carried, or the material it's made out of. There are also specific types of bags for different occupations and activities the user may be involved in throughout the day. Generally, any type of bag can be dressy or casual depending on the design, size, and materials used. This master compilation of types of bags will help you better understand the origins and features of each style.

Additionally, learning the parts of a bag and their purpose will help you better understand what makes these bags distinct from one another. When deciding which features are best for you, it can be helpful to consider where you're going, how you'll get there, what items you want to bring, and what you plan to do when you get there. Also, knowing the parts of a bag can help you understand the construction. Some of the more complex styles may seem intimidating to make, but when they're explained piece by piece, they can be achievable.

Parts of a Bag

CORNERS: Popular types of bag corners include boxed, buckle, dart, folded, grommet, gusset, and metal corners.

POCKETS: The range of bag pockets includes card pockets, covered pockets, expandable slip pockets, expandable zipper pockets, flap pockets, gadget pockets, kiss lock pockets, pleated pockets, slip pockets, zipper pockets, and zipper gusset pockets.

SIDES: A variety of bag side styles include accordion, gusset, panel, side clips, side seam, winged, and zipper-expandable sides.

CLOSURES: Common types of bag closures include buckles, cinch, drawstring, fold-over, frames, full flap, half flap, locks, magnets, open-top, recessed zipper, toggle, top zipper, snaps, and straps.

HANDLES & STRAPS: Choices of handles and straps include acrylic, adjustable, bamboo, beaded, braided, chain, cutout, embroidered, fabric, flat, knotted, loop, metal, plastic, rattan, resin, rolled, rope, shoulder, webbing, wristlet, and wooden.

Accordion Bags

An accordion bag features expandable sides or sections that fold open and closed like an accordion. This style of bag is made up of several small bags, compartments, or pockets stitched together.

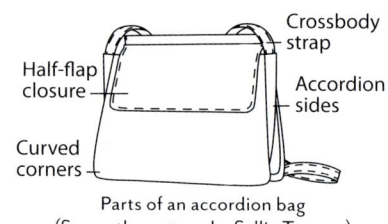

Parts of an accordion bag
(Samantha pattern by Sallie Tomato)

Backpacks, Daypacks & Rucksacks

A backpack is used for carrying items on the back. Traditionally, backpacks feature padded, adjustable shoulder straps. They also contain a variety of compartments and pockets to keep items organized and secure. It's important to note that a backpack is designed to hold more items than a daypack, which is a lighter, more compact version of a backpack. A rucksack is a backpack with a buckle strap closure, many outer pockets, and often a top flap or roll top.

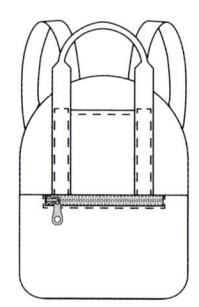

Connie, pattern by Sallie Tomato

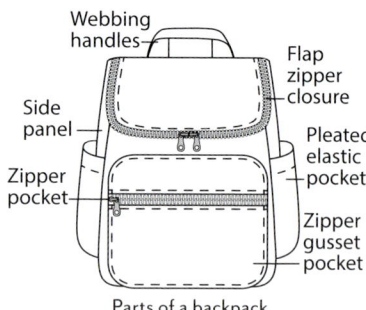

Parts of a backpack

12 ESSENTIAL BAG MAKING REFERENCE TOOL

Baguette

A baguette is a small, long, narrow bag that resembles a loaf of French bread. It features a short shoulder strap and an iconic flap closure. This compact bag rose in popularity in the late 1990s. Baguette bags differ from barrel bags in that they are meant to lie flat.

Carrie, pattern by Sallie Tomato

Barrel Bags

A barrel bag has a barrel-shaped silhouette and features a top zipper closure. Barrel bags are normally handheld, but some have crossbody straps. Depending on the design, the barrel bag can be a popular style for both larger duffle bags and smaller handbags.

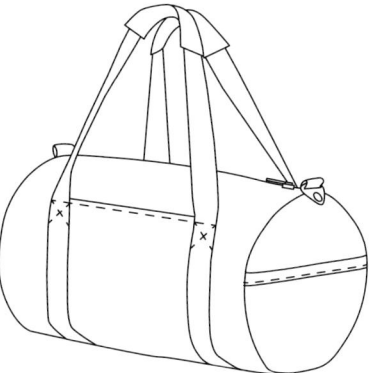

Isla, pattern by Sallie Tomato

Bowling Bags

As its name suggests, the bowling bag was inspired by bags used to carry bowling balls, shoes, and other equipment. Modern bowling bag designs feature a sleek, curved silhouette and short handles along the top; the bag is slipped over the forearm and carried at the elbow.

Bracelet & Wristlet Bags

A bracelet or wristlet bag is meant to be worn around the wrist or held in the hand. Often a short fabric strap is attached to the top or side of the bag; however, modern bags with large bracelet hardware or metal handles are currently trending. This style of bag is more convenient to hold than a clutch.

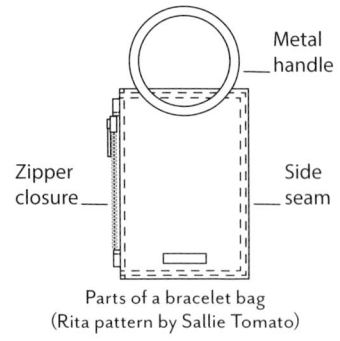

Parts of a bracelet bag
(Rita pattern by Sallie Tomato)

Bucket Bags

A bucket bag is shaped like a bucket. It usually has an open top with a drawstring closure and a shoulder strap. Its roomy interior was originally meant to carry champagne bottles, but this style of bag is now common for everyday wear. This self-standing bag has a firm bottom and often soft sides so it can easily expand open and cinch closed again.

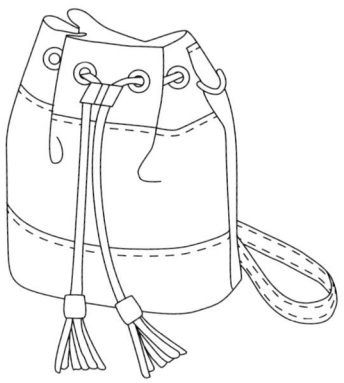

Magnolia, pattern by Sallie Tomato

Camera Bags

Camera bags are designed to be compact and are padded to safely hold a camera, additional lenses, and other accessories. Functionality is the priority for most camera bags; however, some are designed to be more stylish, so it's not as obvious that camera gear is inside. Generally, camera bags feature a top-loading opening for easy access and are carried over the shoulder or in the hand.

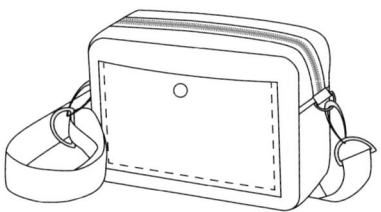

Stewart, pattern by Sallie Tomato

Canteen Bags

A canteen bag is a round, stiff bag that resembles a water flask. Traditionally, it was used as a container for drinking water. The modern-day canteen bag features a structured, circular shape; a long, adjustable strap; and often a tassel.

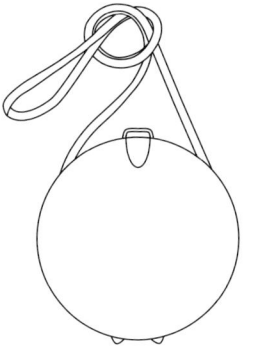

Daisy, pattern by Sallie Tomato

Clutches

Clutches are normally small-sized bags with no handles or straps. This style of bag must be carried in the hand or under the arm. Clutches are designed to be compact and carry minimal essentials. This style of bag is typically carried at formal gatherings or while running quick errands.

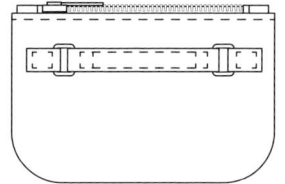

Companion Mini, pattern by Sallie Tomato

Crossbody & Sling Bags

Historically, crossbody and sling bags were known as utility bags and were used to hold small tools or mail. This centuries-old design remains popular and is now available in many styles and sizes. Crossbody and sling bags feature a long, adjustable strap and a flap or zipper closure, and they are generally small in size. This style is worn across the body and rests on the hip. The bag's compact, convenient size and hands-free design have made it a sought-after style for generations.

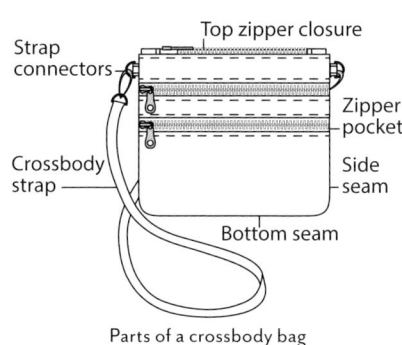

Parts of a crossbody bag
(Zippy pattern by Sallie Tomato)

Diaper Bags

A diaper bag is designed for storing and organizing baby items such as diapers, bottles, toys, and clothing. This style of bag features numerous pockets, compartments, pull-out changing pads, and sometimes even insulated areas for food and drinks. Diaper bags come in a variety of styles, including handbag, backpack, and messenger bag versions, so parents can carry baby items in a way that's most comfortable for their lifestyle.

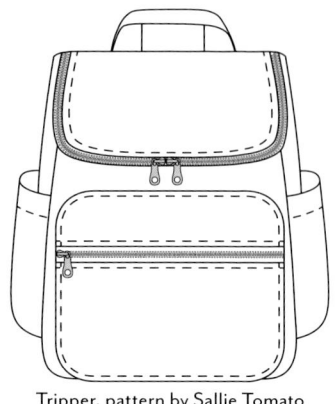

Tripper, pattern by Sallie Tomato

Doctor's Bags

A doctor's bag features a wide-opening top with an interior purse frame. The interior frame gives this style of bag a boxy shape and provides the user with easy access to the many items that can be stored inside for travel. The exterior often features a flat bottom, multiple pockets, and shorter straps. Traditionally, this style of bag was used for in-home visits by physicians.

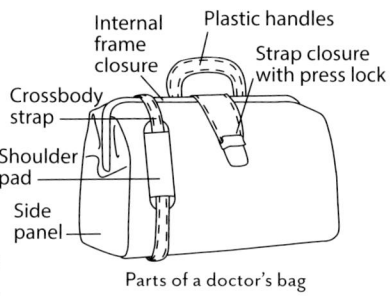

Parts of a doctor's bag

Dopp Kits & Cosmetic Bags

Dopp kits and cosmetic bags are used for transporting essentials such as toiletries, cosmetics, and grooming supplies while traveling. These portable bags feature a small, boxy design and are popular among men and women alike. They are often made out of materials that are durable and easy to clean, such as leather, vinyl, or canvas, and feature a zipper closure.

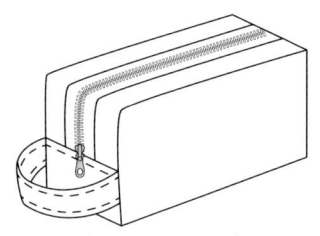

Box Pouch from Create with Cork Fabric, pattern by Sallie Tomato

Drawstring Bags

A drawstring bag has a simple design with a drawstring closure. This bag is lightweight and is often constructed out of durable fabrics such as ripstop and canvas. It's a popular bag for everyday use among students, athletes, and kids.

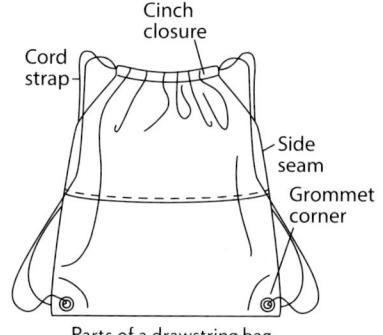

Parts of a drawstring bag
(Burkette pattern by Sallie Tomato)

Duffle Bags

Duffle bags are traditionally large and lightweight, feature multiple pockets, and are carried in the hand or over the shoulder. They are considered ideal for travel or for use by athletes because of their generous carrying capacity.

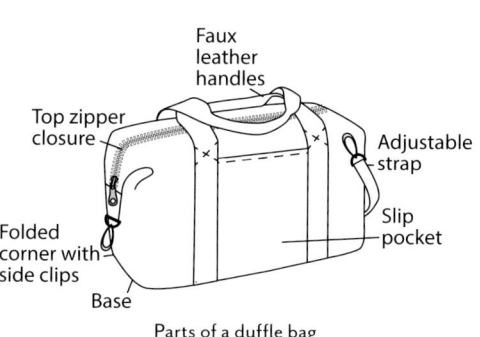

Parts of a duffle bag
(Casey pattern by Sallie Tomato)

Handbags

The handbag is a versatile style of bag that comes in a variety of shapes and sizes. Designs include various closures, handles, pockets, hardware, and other unique features. There have been many iconic handbags throughout history. Handbags are used for carrying daily essentials. This style is carried in the hand or over the shoulder.

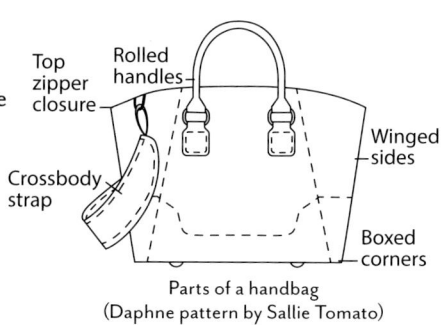

Parts of a handbag
(Daphne pattern by Sallie Tomato)

TYPES OF BAGS & BAG COMPOSITION   17

Hobo Bags

Hobo bags feature a casual, slouchy silhouette. This design is often paired with Bohemian style. Hobo bags commonly have a soft or flexible body, a curved shape, and handles with a long strap drop so they can be carried over the shoulder.

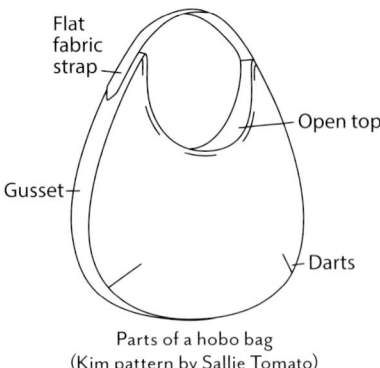

Parts of a hobo bag
(Kim pattern by Sallie Tomato)

Insulated Bags

Insulated bags are useful for keeping food and beverages hot or cold for an extended period of time during transport. This type of bag has an inner layer made of thermal insulating material to reflect heat back toward the source. Some examples of insulated bags include lunch bags, coolers, water bottle carriers, grocery bags, casserole carriers, backpacks, and diaper bags.

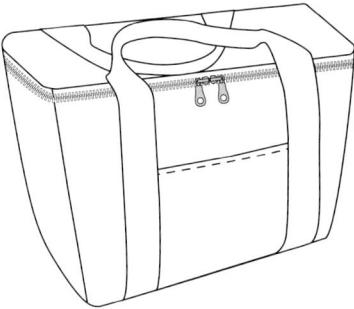

Hudson, pattern by Sallie Tomato

Laptop, Briefcase & Portfolio Bags

Laptop, briefcase, and portfolio bags feature special compartments to store a laptop, tablet, books, important documents, and other work- or school-related items. They are commonly narrow, hard-sided or padded box-shaped bags with carrying handles and sometimes a crossbody strap.

The Morning Post, pattern by Sallie Tomato

Messenger Bags

A messenger bag has a rectangular shape and is large enough to carry papers and books. Typically, this style of bag has a flap closure and a wide strap designed for carrying a lot of weight and is worn across the body. Messenger bags are used by both men and women.

Henderson, pattern by Sallie Tomato

Packing Cubes

Packing cubes are available in a variety of shapes and sizes. They are used for organizing clothes, toiletries, and other personal items while traveling or commuting. They are often made out of breathable fabrics that are easy to clean, such as mesh and ripstop.

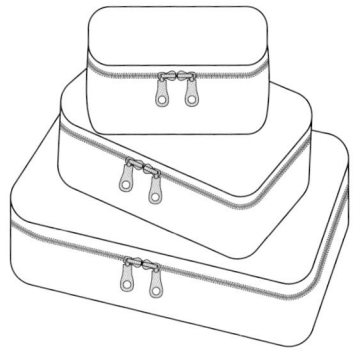

Carlton, pattern by Sallie Tomato

Pouches

Pouches are normally smaller bags with a top zipper closure. Most pouches are handheld, but some have a wrist strap. Pouches are generally used to organize items within larger bags, suitcases, or even bathroom cabinets or craft rooms.

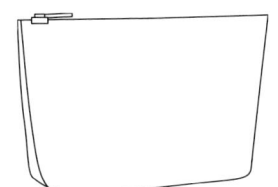

Carry Along, pattern by Sallie Tomato

Saddle Bags

A saddle bag is a small, rounded crossbody bag with a flap closure. These bags are typically made out of leather. Historically, this type of bag was hung from a saddle on a horse, over the rear wheel of a bicycle, or on the seat of a motorcycle.

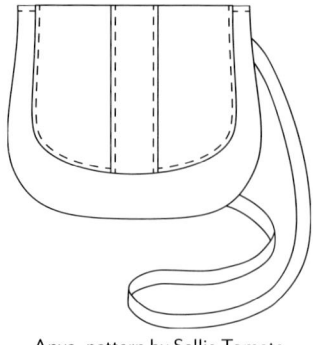

Anya, pattern by Sallie Tomato

Shoulder Bags

A shoulder bag is any type of bag that is worn using a single strap over the shoulder. The designation is a widely used term that can apply to multiple bag styles. Shoulder bags can vary in size and design features.

Sachi, pattern designed by Meme Bete for Sallie Tomato

Specialty Bags

A few examples of specialty bags include musical instrument bags, garment bags, golf bags, and medical bags. Specialty bags are often used in certain occupations or for hobbies.

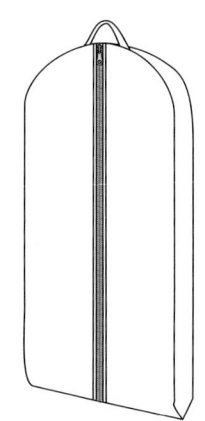

Tote Bags

Tote bags are medium- to large-sized bags with two straps. They typically have an open top with either a magnetic snap or zipper closure or even no closure at all. A tote bag has a flat bottom and tall sides. Totes are often called shopping bags or beach bags.

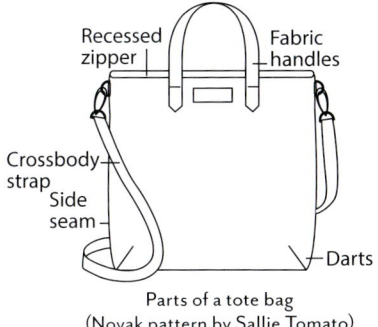

Parts of a tote bag
(Novak pattern by Sallie Tomato)

Waist Bags

Waist bags are designed to be worn around the waist and hold daily essentials. This type of bag features an adjustable strap that can sometimes be attached to a belt. Other names for waist bags include belt bag, bum bag, fanny pack, and hip pack.

Ferris, pattern by Sallie Tomato

BAG CARE

Cleaning & Conditioning

To extend the longevity of the fabric, it's important to clean and condition your bags regularly to prevent stains, scuffs, odors, and general wear and tear. Taking a few minutes to clean both the inside and outside of the bags is important to restore and maintain handles, corners, and frequently used areas.

Some bag care supplies and storage options include mild soap, polish, shine cloths, microfiber cloths, leather conditioners, stain and water-repellant spray, dust bags, storage boxes, and silica gel packets. Refer to the cleaner and conditioner product instructions for exact uses and instructions.

Start by emptying out the contents of the bag. Use a lint roller or a vacuum with a fabric brush attachment to remove dust and debris. Clean the bag inside and outside with a soft cloth and a mild cleaning solution such as dish soap or a small amount of laundry detergent. Gently massage stubborn areas, and then use a damp cloth to wipe off the soap. Machine washing and bleach are not recommended for bags and accessories.

Let the bag dry naturally, upside down so any water drips from the top of the bag. Once it is mostly dry, apply a conditioning cream or waterproofer such as Scotchgard (depending on the material) and wipe off any excess. Conditioning cream is generally used on leather to prevent it from drying out, staining, and cracking. Scotchgard is a great option for woven fabric and cork fabric bags to protect them from water, oils, and salt. Special care kits are available that include a cleaning solution; conditioning cream; and proper sponges, cloths, and brushes. The cleaning process should be carried out about every three months for bags that are used daily, or about every six to nine months for special-occasion bags, to keep them protected. To treat specific types of stains, search online for more detailed treatment options based on the fabric and the cause of the stain.

Organizing & Care Accessories

- Use dust covers or old pillowcases to store and protect your bags when they're not being used.
- Avoid a messy bag by using a purse organizer insert to provide additional pockets and compartments, which can be interchanged between bags.
- Pouches are useful accessories inside bags for storing cosmetics, pens, and food.
- Attach a purse hook to a handle or strap to allow you to hang your bag from doorknobs, shopping carts, bathroom stall hooks, and more.
- A key clip is a useful accessory to prevent your keys from getting buried beneath other items inside your bag. Make your own key clip by simply attaching a swivel hook to a gate ring and clipping the gate ring to a handle, strap, or ring on a bag.
- Add a bag base to help maintain the bag's shape. A bag base can be added after the project is completed. Custom sizes and shapes are available to fit your handmade or ready-made bags. ❖

Top 10 Bag Care Tips

1. Be mindful of your fabric and interfacing choices for lasting results. Select materials that are durable and will hold up over time. If you choose a more delicate fabric, make sure to properly interface, stabilize, and care for the fabric to keep it in its best condition.

2. Use a quality thread for project construction! It's the worst feeling when your project starts coming apart, so don't settle for something that may not withstand use.

3. Reinforce your bag's seams and stress areas whenever possible. Extra stitching or the addition of hardware can increase durability.

4. During the project construction, reduce bulk in the seam allowances whenever possible. Some seam allowances should not be trimmed down—for example, if additional pieces are going to be attached to them. In most cases, cutting notches within the seam allowance, trimming away just the interfacing layer, or trimming bulk from corners is enough to help reduce bulk and result in a smooth finish.

5. Take advantage of the wide variety of notions available to help with construction and enhance the final results of your project. Besides the basics, my go-to notions include a Teflon zipper foot, a narrow zipper foot, sewing clips, basting tape, basting spray, a stiletto, a hot hemmer, chalk, and a seam roller.

6. Don't overfill your bag! Many of us are guilty of carrying too many items or items that are too heavy. Doing so can cause damage to your bag because of the excess stress on pockets, straps, and fabrics. And it adds strain to your shoulders, neck, and back. So be sure to choose the proper size and style for what you need to carry.

7. To avoid accidental stains, place cosmetics, pens, and food inside sealed pouches before putting them inside your bag.

8. Be mindful of where you place your bags and accessories while shopping, at restaurants, in the car, in public restrooms, and at other destinations throughout your day. Make sure the surface won't scuff, stain, or damage your bag in any way.

9. Always spot-test a cleaning method in an inconspicuous location, such as on the inside of the bag or the outside base, before using it on the entire bag.

10. Store your bags properly to prevent damage over time. Stuff your bags while you're not using them to help maintain their shape. Don't leave your bags in direct sunlight, as it can cause the fabric to fade. Also, use a dust cover to keep your bags clean. ◇

FABRICS & INTERFACING

With such a wide range of fabrics and interfacings available on the market, it can be difficult to understand the differences and choose a good fit for your project. In bag making, it's important to choose fabrics that will withstand everyday wear. Some fabrics may be tempting to use because of the designs or textures, but keep in mind their durability and weight. Often, it's the fabric and interfacing selection that can make or break a project. This chapter contains a thoughtful list of fabrics and interfacings along with their common applications, thread and needle recommendations, and basic care instructions to guide your decision-making when selecting fabrics.

Canvas

Canvas is a woven fabric typically made out of cotton. Canvas is durable, and some types are water-resistant or even waterproof. This fabric is ideal for projects that will see a lot of use, such as bags, clothing, coverings, upholstery, and outdoor items. Use a size 90/14 universal or jeans needle, depending on the weight of the canvas.

Cork

Cork fabric consists of a thin layer of 100% cork adhered to a fabric support backing, which is often a blend of polyester, cotton, and polyurethane. Cork fabric can be found in a variety of thicknesses, qualities, textures, prints, and colors. Quality cork fabric is soft, smooth, and pliable. This fabric is sustainable, durable, antimicrobial, hypoallergenic, and stain-resistant. Cork fabric is commonly used to make bags, wallets, accents on clothing, craft projects, shoes, and upholstery. Use a size 80/12 universal, microtex, or topstitch needle.

Cotton

Cotton is a woven fabric made from a natural fiber derived from cotton plants. There are four different types of cotton fabric: pima, Egyptian, upland, and organic. Each type has its own quality characteristics and best uses. Cotton fabric is used for making clothing, bedding and quilts, bags, and home decor. Keep in mind that cotton is usually too light for most bag projects, but it is suitable for linings. Use a 70/11 or 80/12 universal or quilting needle when sewing with cotton.

Denim

Denim is a durable cotton fabric made using a twill weave. There are six different types of denim fabric: indigo, stretch, crushed, acid-wash, raw, and Sanforized. Each type has its own characteristics, treatment, and best uses. Denim is used for making clothing, bags, and home decor. Use a 90/14 or 100/16 denim or jeans needle, depending on the weight of the denim being sewn.

Essex Linen

Essex linen is a medium-weight woven fabric made from a cotton and linen blend. Because of its softness, luxurious drape, and sturdy texture, it's commonly used for apparel, quilts, bags, and upholstery. Use a size 70/11 or 80/12 universal or quilting needle to sew Essex linen.

Faux Leather

There are two major types of faux leather: vinyl-based and polyurethane-based. Vinyl-based faux leather is basically dyed plastic. Examples are marine vinyl and clear vinyl, which are very stiff. Polyurethane-based faux leather is made by coating a natural fabric such as cotton or polyester and then treating it to look like real leather. This type of faux leather is softer and more flexible and breathable than vinyl-based leather. Faux leather is used for a variety of projects, including bags, wallets, upholstery, home decor, craft projects, and garments. A size 90/14 or 80/12 universal or denim needle works best when sewing through faux leather.

Flannel

Flannel is a soft woven fabric made from wool, cotton or synthetic fiber. Its cozy, soft touch comes from brushing or the loosely woven fiber construction. This type of fabric is more common in bags used in the fall and winter because of its warm touch and the range of plaid patterns available. Since flannel is a popular choice for cold-weather use, making a coordinating flannel scarf, hand warmers, apparel, or other accessories to match a bag can create a fun ensemble. Use a 100/16 or 90/14 universal needle for sewing with flannel, depending on the weight of the fabric.

Fur & Faux Fur

Authentic fur is obtained from animals such as mink, cows, and rabbits. Genuine fur is expensive and is becoming less popular than faux fur, or synthetic fur, options. Faux fur is typically a knitted fabric made from a blend of acrylic and polyester fibers. It can vary in type, texture, color, softness, and pile, which is the height of the raised fibers. Each type of faux fur has its own characteristics, such as pile and nap, or the direction the fur pile lies. Use a 90/14 or 100/16 universal needle for knitted faux fur, or an 80/12 nonstick needle for flocked faux fur.

Kraft-tex

Kraft-tex is a durable fabric made from paper. There are two types of kraft-tex: original unwashed and prewashed. Both types soften and crinkle with handling and washing. Kraft-tex is used for craft projects, bags, mixed-media arts, home decor, and bookmaking. When sewing with kraft-tex, use a longer stitch length and an embroidery or 80/12 sharp sewing machine needle.

Laminated Cotton

Laminated cotton is cotton fabric that is coated with nontoxic, water-based polyurethane. Laminated cotton is durable, waterproof, soft, and lightweight. It's used for making bags, aprons, tablecloths, diaper covers, upholstery, and more. An 80/12 universal needle works best for sewing through laminated cotton.

Leather

Genuine leather is made from animal hides or skins. Leather is durable, wrinkle-resistant, soft, and available in a variety of textures, colors, and weights. Leather can be treated and tanned with vegetable matter or chromium salts. This material is used for bags, clothing, shoes, upholstery, and bookmaking. Use a longer stitch length and a leather needle in an appropriate size for the weight of the leather. Genuine leather is nonwoven and can be very thick to sew through, so an industrial sewing machine or hand stitching will yield the best results.

Mesh

Mesh is a knitted fabric typically made from polyester or nylon. The material is constructed with evenly spaced openings that allow it to be breathable, lightweight, and flexible. Mesh fabric can have a variety of applications, depending on the size and shape of the openings and the blend of synthetic fibers. Mesh may be used for sports apparel and equipment; camping, hunting, and fishing gear; casual apparel; and technology and travel accessories. Use a shorter stitch length and a jersey or ballpoint needle so the tip slides between the fibers, allowing the fabric to remain stretchable.

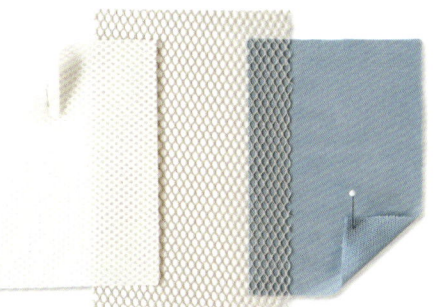

Oilcloth

Oilcloth is a sturdy fabric such as duck or canvas that is coated with PVC. Oilcloth is durable and waterproof and doesn't fray along the cut edges. Because it's easy to clean and has a sturdy drape, oilcloth is commonly used for tablecloths, place mats, lunch bags, and equipment covers. Use a size 90/14 universal or denim needle and a longer stitch length to sew oilcloth.

Sequins

Sequin fabric is a woven, stretch, lace, or mesh fabric with shaped plastic pieces called sequins that have been sewn in place. The sequins may be stitched or adhered flat to the fabric or attached with a single stitch so they can move freely. Sequins can vary in size, shape, color, and nap. This type of material is often used for dance apparel, formal wear, home decor, and bags. It's important to remove sequins from the seam allowance and sew using a 70/11 microtex needle.

Suede & Microsuede

Suede is a type of leather that is made from the underside of the animal hide. Microsuede is faux suede that is made from polyester fabric with a suede-like texture. Suede and microsuede are known for their soft, smooth appearance and drape. Both are very durable and pliable, making them ideal for footwear, accessories, clothing, bags, and upholstery. However, suede can be difficult to keep clean and is easily damaged by water. Microsuede is often water-resistant and easier to care for. Use an 80/12 leather needle for sewing genuine suede or an 80/12 universal needle for microsuede.

Ripstop

Ripstop is a lightweight woven fabric often made of nylon, cotton, or polyester. The material is manufactured in a crosshatch pattern so the fibers are interwoven, making it resistant to tearing and ripping. Some types of ripstops have a waterproof coating, which is ideal for outdoor apparel, equipment coverings, bags, utility items, and upholstery. Use a size 70/11 or 80/12 universal needle.

Velvet & Velveteen

Velvet is a smooth, dense, short-pile fabric typically made from silk, rayon, acetate, polyester, or a blend of these fibers. Velveteen is less dense, stiffer than velvet, and made from cotton. These types of fabrics add a lush touch and dimension to clothing, bags, formal wear, upholstery, bedding, and home decor. Use a 70/11 microtex or stretch needle for sewing with these materials.

Vinyl

Vinyl is a nonwoven fabric made from synthetic materials (a type of plastic). Vinyl is available in a wide variety of colors, finishes, patterns, and weights. Vinyl is often used for craft projects, outdoor and athletic items, raincoats, and bags. A 90/14 vinyl, leather, denim, or nonstick needle is recommended, with a longer stitch length.

Waxed Canvas

Waxed canvas is a sturdy woven fabric that has been saturated with wax. Waxed canvas is durable, flexible, and water-resistant, and it gains a weathered appearance the more it is folded and handled over time. This type of material is usually used to make outdoor clothing, coverings, and a wide range of bags. Use a size 100/16 sharp sewing machine needle for sewing waxed canvas.

Interfacing & Support Materials

WHAT IS INTERFACING?

Interfacing is a material used to add shape, strength, and structure to fabric. Interfacing gives you the ability to add additional stability to certain projects that require support or shaping, such as bags. There are three main types of interfacing; woven, nonwoven, and knit. Additional types of interfacing include fleece batting, foam, and hair canvas. All these types of interfacing come in different weights, colors, and applications, including fusible and sew-in versions.

In addition to the desired shape or structure, the type of fabric used in a project will help determine which interfacing to choose. A general rule of thumb is to choose a dark interfacing when using a dark fabric, and a light interfacing when using a light fabric. Always read the manufacturer's instructions before applying any interfacing to your fabric. Also, test the interfacing on a scrap of fabric before using it for a project.

TYPES & BEST USES OF INTERFACING

Fleece & Batting Interfacing

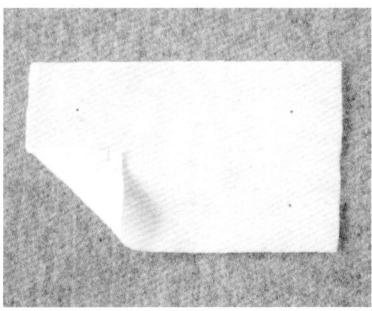

Fleece and batting interfacing are soft and flexible options for adding body and stability to projects. For bag making, a low loft is often best because it provides the least amount of bulk in the seams and a finished look. Use fleece or batting in between the exterior and lining layers for a more relaxed appearance, or use it when working with firmer exterior fabrics, such as cork, faux leather, or kraft-tex, that don't need as much added stability.

Foam Interfacing

Foam interfacing is a go-to option for stabilizing bags for many reasons: it's lightweight, soft, formable, it maintains its shape, and is easy to sew. This type of interfacing is unique because it's composed of a layer of napped spun lace (foam) between polyester fabric layers. Foam interfacing is machine washable and can be used with all types of fabrics. Use foam interfacing in between the exterior and lining layers of your bag for a sturdy appearance.

Fusible Interfacing

Fusible interfacing has an adhesive backing that bonds to fabric with the heat of an iron. This type of interfacing is fast and easy to apply. Most fusible interfacing has small, rough dots of adhesive, but some types have a shiny adhesive, so you're able to see or feel which is the fusible side. A disadvantage of some fusible interfacing is that the fabric may crease easily, and it can be difficult to iron away any creases after the project is complete. Fusible interfacing can be used on any fabric that can be ironed. It's a convenient option to avoid machine basting the interfacing to your fabric. Fusible interfacing is available as both woven and non-woven versions.

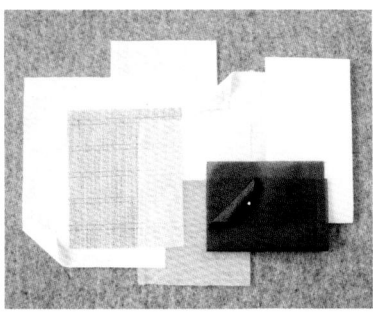

Hair Canvas Interfacing

Hair canvas interfacing is a woven interfacing used to ensure crisp details and firm control in areas on bags and apparel. It's a natural cloth commonly composed of a blend of cotton, rayon, polyester, wool, and horse hair or goat hair. It holds its shape very well when stiffness is desired. Use hair canvas with medium-weight to heavyweight fabrics.

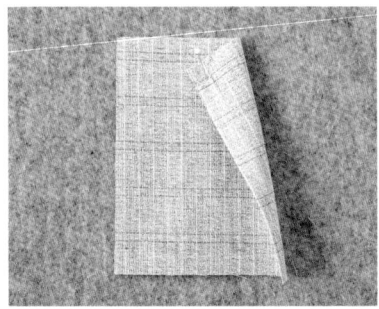

Heat-Reflective Fleece Interfacing

Heat-reflective fleece is a polyester fleece and polyethylene film that maintains both hot and cold temperatures by reflecting hot or cold temperatures back to the source rather than allowing it to pass through the fabric. It's used for a variety of projects, including insulated bags, lunch carriers, pot holders, tea cozies, oven mitts, blankets, slippers, window coverings, and more.

Knit Interfacing

Knit interfacing is soft and flexible. It has a crosswise stretch. This type of interfacing is best used on woven fabrics to achieve a softer shape or to maintain stretch after the interfacing is applied. Knit interfacing is most commonly used in apparel sewing.

Nonwoven Interfacing

Nonwoven interfacing does not have a grain. It's made of bonded or felted fibers. This type of interfacing is very easy to use since it can be cut and used in any direction, and it won't fray. Nonwoven interfacing can be used on all types of fabric except stretch fabric. Use nonwoven interfacing on craft and home decor projects that need certain areas to be very firm or stiff or left with a raw edge. It can also be used on bags to stabilize the straps or base, but it has a tendency to make the fabric appear creased or wrinkled with use.

Sew-In Interfacing

Sew-in interfacing is attached to the fabric with stitching. An advantage of using sew-in interfacing is that it will allow the fabric to maintain its natural shape and drape. Examples of fabrics to best use sew-in interfacing on include lace, mesh, fabrics with a lot of texture, and heat-sensitive fabrics.

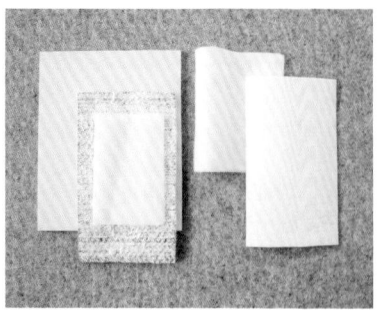

Woven Interfacing

Woven interfacing has a lengthwise and crosswise grain. It's important to match the grain of the interfacing with the grain of the fabric to make sure the interfacing works as intended. Woven interfacing, which tends to have a stronger bond and is more durable than nonwoven interfacing, is commonly used on all types of fabric. Use woven interfacing on projects that will be handled or washed, such as bags, apparel, and some home decor projects, for the most natural look and feel.

TYPES & BEST USES OF SUPPORT MATERIALS

Acrylic Bag Base

An acrylic bag base is set into the bottom of a bag as firm support to maintain the bag's shape. These bases are usually made from acrylic, but they can also be made from plexiglass or plastic. Custom sizes and shapes are available to fit your handmade or ready-made bags. They are the firmest support option, but they can also add a lot of weight to your bag.

Fabric or Plastic Bag Base

Fabric or plastic bag bases are a thin, lightweight option for stabilizing the base of a bag. They are often more flexible than an acrylic base. They can be added in between the exterior and lining layers or simply set inside the bag after project completion. A fabric base is typically made from leather or felt.

Metal Frames

An internal or external metal frame can be added to the top, sides, or bottom of a bag to help maintain the bag's shape. Frames can be screwed on, sewn on, glued on, or inserted in between the exterior and lining layers, depending on the design.

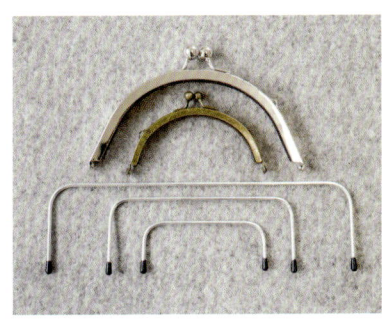

Piping & Cording

Piping and cording are handy for adding structure, stability, and detail. They're often found on high-end bags and luxury goods. Piping is a strip of fabric folded and stitched over a cord. Cording is a decorative cord with fabric woven to it. Adding piping or cording is a way to structure your project while achieving a professional look without much extra effort. Sew piping or cording into seams on bags, apparel, or home decor.

PART TWO
Making Bags

HARDWARE

Hardware may seem intimidating; however, most purse hardware is surprisingly simple to install and can instantly transform a bag's look from homemade to designer. Customize bags and accessories with simple or unique hardware that can be functional or just for adornment. Certain types of hardware can also be used to reinforce stress points on bags, to make them last longer and withstand frequent use. Make sure your fabrics are properly interfaced and stabilized before and after inserting hardware.

There are generally two qualities of purse hardware finishes: rolling finish and hanging finish. Rolling finish is an inexpensive, lower-quality plating. It doesn't look as shiny and doesn't last as long as a hanging finish. Purse hardware with a rolling finish has a very fine layer of color that tends to rub off quickly. Hanging finish is a high-quality plating method. Each item is individually dipped and later sprayed with lacquer for a long-lasting coat. This process is more labor-intensive and therefore more expensive; however, you can feel and see the difference compared to the rolling finish.

Bag making can be very time-consuming, so it's important to invest in purse hardware that will last. Sallie Tomato is a great resource for hardware, tutorials, and patterns, offering a growing selection of styles and types in an array of finishes to choose from. To have the best experience using hardware, you'll want to learn the types of hardware and their applications. Several types of hardware in this section include basic installation tutorials.

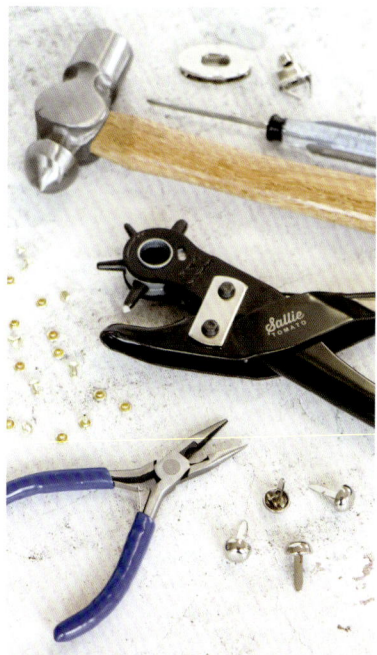

Bag Feet

Bag feet come in a variety of shapes and sizes and are normally installed with screws, prongs, or rivets. Bag feet help prevent the bottom of your bag from getting dirty. Also, they add stability and can even be used as embellishments.

The size refers to the outer width of the bag foot.

Lauren, pattern designed by Sallie Tomato

INSTALLING BAG FEET

Mark the placement for each bag foot according to your pattern's instructions. At each placement mark, cut a small slit with scissors or a seam ripper, or use a rotary punch on the smallest setting to punch a small hole. Insert the prongs of a bag foot through each opening, from the right side to the wrong side. On the wrong side, place a washer over the prongs. Bend each

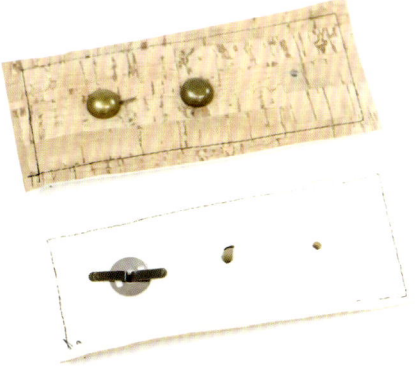

of the prongs away from the center. Add a drop of permanent glue over the prongs. If desired, fuse a scrap of interfacing over the prongs to help prevent future wear on your lining fabric.

HARDWARE

Buckles

Buckles are popular components for bag making and are available in a variety of shapes, sizes, and styles. Buckles may be more useful in certain areas than others, depending on the strap or handle attachment and buckle function. The size of a buckle refers to the inside measurement (the strap accommodation width) rather than the outer dimension.

CENTER BAR

Center bar buckles are often rectangular or square shaped with a bar along the center and a pin attached. This type of hardware allows the length of belts and straps to be adjusted. The pin attached to the center bar pokes through a hole in the belt or strap to secure the buckle in place. This type of hardware is often used on bags, belts, and shoes.

HEEL BAR

Heel bar buckles are often rectangular or square shaped with a bar along one end and a pin attached. This type of hardware allows the length of belts and straps to be adjusted. The pin attached to the end of the buckle pokes through a hole in the belt or strap to secure the buckle in place. This type of hardware is often used on bags, belts, and shoes.

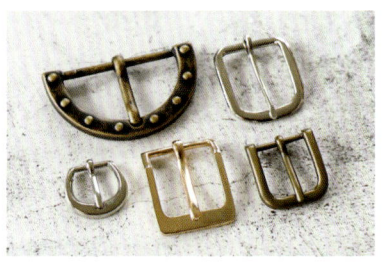

LADDER LOCK

Ladder lock buckles are designed to hold under tension and release when the front tab is lifted. They allow the length and tension of straps to be adjusted. Single-sided ladder buckles are easily adjustable from one end. This makes one-handed adjustment easy, whether releasing or tightening. This type of hardware is ideal for backpack straps, fanny packs, hip packs, and other bags that require an adjustable strap.

Shaw, pattern designed by Sallie Tomato

ROLLER

Roller buckles have a cylinder roller attached to one side of the buckle, and a pin opposite of the roller. The roller allows heavy-duty straps and belts to slide easily through the buckle. It also protects the strap or belt from wear when the buckle is fastened. This hardware is commonly used for concealed carry and a wide range of belts.

SIDE RELEASE

Side release buckles can be opened and closed with one hand by squeezing the side clips. This type of hardware is commonly made out of metal or plastic. Most buckles of this type are used for securing straps and belts, but some are used to tighten and lock under tension. This hardware is used for dog collars, backpacks, belts, and other straps.

SLIDER

Slider buckles allow the length of straps and belts to be adjusted by feeding the strap through the slots. These buckles are also called tri-glides, slip locks, 3-bar sliders, or butterfly buckles. Slider buckles are commonly used for lightweight bags, dog collars, fanny packs, and belts.

Chain

Chain is a series of links used for connecting or embellishment. Chain can add a luxurious accent to bags and accessories, but it can also have a functional purpose as strap hardware and closure details. Typically, a chain is used as decor or as the bag's strap. It's available in various sizes, shapes, and thicknesses.

Conchos

Conchos are shapes and designs, usually metal, used to embellish bags, belts, saddles, and more. These adornments are typically sewn, threaded, or screwed into place. Conchos often feature engravings, crystals, and/or stamped designs.

Cord Locks

Cord locks, also known as drawstring adjusters, are toggles with single or double holes. The spring button allows a drawstring or cord to be cinched tight and then loosened. Drawstring adjusters are used for bags, backpacks, pants, jackets, and more.

Frames

INTERNAL FRAMES

Internal frames are concealed between the exterior and lining materials of bags and luggage to add shape, support, and structure. This type of hardware holds bags open wide for easy access to and visibility of items inside.

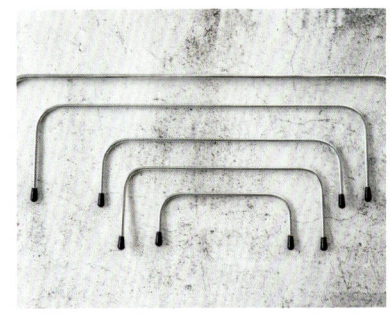

KISS LOCK

Kiss lock purse frames feature a large ball clasp that locks when pressed together and opens when twisted apart. This type of frame is usually installed by pushing the top edge of a bag inside the channel of the frame and sewing, clamping, and/or gluing it in place. Kiss lock frames are used for bags, clutches, and coin purses.

Clara, pattern designed by Sallie Tomato

HARDWARE 45

Grommets & Eyelets

Grommets and eyelets are used to reinforce a pierced hole in a piece of fabric. Once installed, grommets and eyelets are used for attaching straps, leather lacing, or rope, as well as for cinching bags and covers. Grommets are larger, are usually installed with force or screws, and

are typically used for heavy-duty fabrics, outdoor equipment, and bags. Eyelets are smaller, are usually installed with prongs by force, and are used for lightweight bags, apparel, and delicate fabrics.

Key Fobs

Key fob hardware is a rectangular clamp piece with a split ring attached at the top. This type of hardware is used to create key fobs, lanyards, and other handheld or wrist-carried accessories. The hardware is clamped or screwed to a looped strap or webbing for

convenient carrying, and keys or other small accessories are attached to the split ring.

Labels

Labels are used to adorn bags, apparel, and accessories. Often installed with prongs or screws, they are available in a variety of shapes, fonts, colors, and materials. Designers and makers use labels to promote their brand or country of origin.

Locks & Closures

CHANNELED LOCKS

Channeled locks are most often installed by pushing the flap edge of a bag inside the channel of the lock and screwing, clamping, and/or gluing it in place. Channeled locks are used to secure the flaps of handbags, backpack flaps, wallets, and other bags.

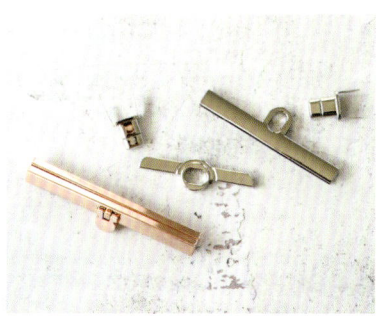

DRAW BOLTS

A drawbolt lock is a two-piece closure that clamps tightly together when the lever is hooked over the clasp and pushed flat. This type of hardware is nailed, screwed, or riveted in place, so it's usually used on heavy-duty bags and storage containers such as luggage, briefcases, and chests.

FLIP LOCKS

Flip locks, also called drop locks, are made up of two pieces: a base plate and a flip unit. To secure this lock, the flip unit is inserted into the slot of the base plate and flipped down to prevent the two units from pulling apart. Flip locks are used to secure pockets, flaps, wallets, and bags.

PIN CLASPS

A pin clasp is a two-piece closure that is secured when the pin is pushed through the hole of the base plate. These closures are not very common, since they are more decorative than functional. Pin clasps are typically used on formal bags such as handbags and clutches.

SQUEEZE LOCKS

Squeeze locks open when the front buttons are squeezed, releasing the top of the lock. This type of hardware is heavy and takes two hands to unlock. Squeeze locks are typically used on formal bags such as handbags and clutches.

SWING CATCHES

A swing catch lock is secured in place by swinging the spiked arm into the base plate. The base plate is often installed with rivets or screws. Swing catches are commonly used on bag flaps, clutches, luggage, and wooden boxes.

TUCK CATCHES

Tuck catches are also called press locks, thumb catches, or tongue locks. This two-piece lock is secured when the tuck unit is compressed and pushed through the slot of the base plate. This hardware comes in a variety of shapes and sizes. Smaller tuck catches are used to secure pocket flaps, clutches, and wallets. Larger locks are used to secure handbag and backpack flaps. Some tuck catches include a key, therefore making them a tuck lock.

TURN LOCKS

Turn locks are made up of two pieces: a base plate and a turn unit. To secure this lock, the turn unit is inserted into the slot of the base plate and twisted to prevent the two units from pulling apart. Turn locks are used to secure pockets, flaps, wallets, and bags.

Monroe, pattern designed by Sallie Tomato

INSTALLING TURN LOCKS

The parts of a turn lock are the turn unit, washer, and base unit, which consists of a faceplate, backplate, and screws.

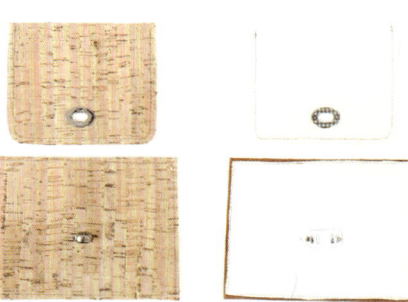

1. Mark the placement for the turn unit on the body or inner piece of the bag, and mark the placement for the base unit on the flap or outer piece. Center the washer over the placement mark for the turn unit and mark the rectangle openings for the prongs. Use scissors or a seam ripper to cut a small slit at each mark.

2. Insert the prongs of the turn unit through the slits from the right side to the wrong side. On the wrong side, place a washer over the prongs. Bend the prongs away from the center. (Pliers may help bend the prongs.) Add a drop of permanent glue over the prongs. If desired, fuse a scrap of interfacing over the prongs to help prevent future wear on your lining fabric.

3. Center the backplate over the placement mark for the base unit and mark the opening and screw holes. Cut out the opening and holes for the screws. Test the fit of the faceplate to see if more fabric needs to be cut away. Position the faceplate over the cut area against the exterior fabric, and the backplate over the cut area against the interior fabric.

4. Screw together.

Magnetic Snaps

INSTALLING MAGNETIC SNAPS

1. Mark the placement for the two halves of the magnetic snap on the lining pieces for each side of the bag. Fuse a scrap of interfacing over the placement marks on the wrong side of the fabric to add stability and prevent future wear. Center a washer over the placement line and mark each rectangle opening. Set the washer aside.

2. Use scissors or a seam ripper to cut a small slit at each mark. On each lining piece, insert the prongs of one-half of the magnetic snap through the slits from the right side to the wrong side. On the wrong side, place a washer over the prongs. Bend the prongs away from the center. Pliers may help bend the prongs.

3. Add a drop of permanent glue over the prongs. If desired, fuse a scrap of interfacing over the prongs to help prevent future wear on your lining fabric.

INVISIBLE

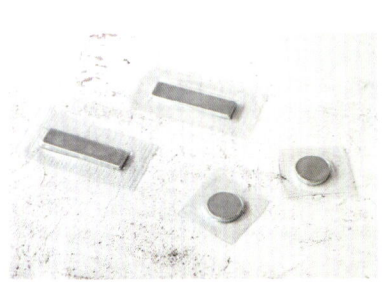

Invisible magnetic snaps are sewn in between the exterior and lining fabrics so the snaps aren't visible from either side of the bag. This style of snap provides a clean, professional finish. Some invisible snaps are very powerful to ensure that the magnets will connect through the fabric.

PRONGED

Pronged magnetic snaps are the most common type of magnetic closure. This style of snap is easily installed with prongs. These snaps are used as closures on pockets, wallets, backpacks, bucket bags, handbags, and more.

SEW-IN

Sew-in magnetic snaps are sewn into place. They are used to secure pockets, wallets, backpacks, and many other varieties of bags. An advantage of sew-in snaps is that they can be installed in any area that needs more security after a bag is completed.

Metal Handles

Metal handles are a durable option for handbag, tote, or wrist bag handles; however, they can add more weight to your bag. They come in a variety of shapes and styles and provide a luxury finish.

Rings

Rings are popular components for bag making and are available in a variety of shapes, sizes, and styles. Ring shapes may be more useful in certain areas than others, depending on the strap or handle attachment. The size of a ring refers to the inner measurement at the widest point.

ARTISAN RINGS

Artisan rings are uniquely shaped or embellished rings. Some artisan rings feature engravings, crystals, or stamped designs.

D-RINGS

D-rings are D-shaped metal or plastic rings used for attaching straps and handles. They are often used in conjunction with a swivel hook. The flat side of the hardware is where the fabric strap, handle, or connector is attached, and the curved side of the hardware is where the swivel hook is attached. The flat side of the D-ring keeps the fabric flat, and the curved side allows the swivel hook to move freely from side to side.

O-RINGS

O-rings are O-shaped metal or plastic rings used for attaching straps and handles. O-rings can also be used as embellishment.

RECTANGLE RINGS

Rectangle rings are rectangular or square-shaped metal or plastic rings. They are commonly used for attaching fabric straps and handles. The two longest edges of the hardware are where the fabric straps, handles, or connectors are attached. These edges keep the folds of the fabric flat and help prevent them from shifting or bunching up.

SPLIT RINGS

Split rings are spiral wire rings that are pressed flat. The spiral can be slightly separated to open the coil and attach keys, pendants, charms, and other objects.

SPRING GATE

Spring gate rings are O-shaped metal rings with a spring gate that opens when pushed. Spring gate rings are useful for attaching straps, handles, unique embellishments, key rings, and other accessories.

TRIANGLE RINGS

Triangle rings are triangle-shaped metal or plastic rings used for attaching straps and handles. Typically, triangle rings have a long, narrow opening along the bottom edge for a strap, and a round opening at the top point for a swivel hook to attach.

Townsend, pattern designed by Sallie Tomato

Rivets & Chicago Screws

Rivets and Chicago screws consist of a post and cap that, once set in place, are used to reinforce or adorn straps, handles, and other areas on bags and wallets.

INSTALLING RIVETS

Determine the correct size of rivet by measuring the thickness of the area where it will be installed and selecting a rivet with a post that is no more than ⅛" (3mm) longer than the thickness. Use a rotary punch or awl to pierce an ⅛" (3mm) diameter hole where the rivet will be installed. Push the post through the hole, and snap the cap on the end of the post. Use a rivet press or hand-setting tools to set the rivet in place.

Snap Fasteners

Snap fasteners are interlocking metal or plastic discs that fasten together when force is applied. Snap fasteners consist of four components and need to be installed with a specific tool. They are used for fastening pockets, flaps, adjustable straps, belts, and more.

INSTALLING SNAP FASTENERS

Parts of a snap fastener from left to right: socket, cap, stud, eyelet.
The socket will be used with the cap. The stud will be used with the eyelet.

1. Use a rotary punch or awl to pierce two holes: one where the cap will be installed and one where the stud will be installed.

2. Position the line snap pieces with the stud and cap against the topside and the eyelet and socket against the underside.

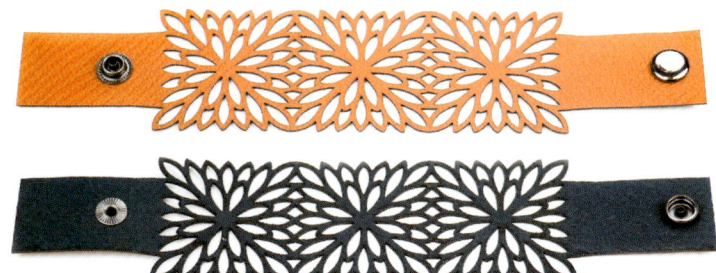

3. Place the cap against the anvil, and the setter in the center of the socket. Tap the setter in place with a hammer to secure the hardware.

4. Place the eyelet on a flat surface or the anvil, and the setter in the center of the stud. Tap the setter in place with a hammer to secure the hardware in place.

HARDWARE 55

Spots

Spots are metal adornments that are installed with a screw or prongs or are riveted in place. Common shapes of spots are dome, barrel, spike, pyramid, and novelty shapes.

Strap Arches

Strap arches are arch-shaped metal trim or connectors used to adorn or secure straps and handles to bags. They are also called arch bridges or strap bridges and are usually installed with screws or prongs.

Tiffany, pattern designed by Sallie Tomato

Strap Connectors

Strap connectors, or anchors, are metal adornments in various shapes that are used to secure straps and handles to bags. They are very strong and durable, with a high-end appearance.

Strap Ends

Strap ends are metal coverings used to conceal the raw ends of straps and handles. They are available in a variety of shapes, sizes, and textures.

Stud Buttons

A stud button consists of a metal post with a spherical top and a screw. Stud buttons are used to securely connect two or more layers of fabric on straps, handles, and belts, and to add stability to bags.

Swivel Hooks

BOLT

A bolt-style swivel hook has a question-mark shape and is opened by pushing down on a trigger. The hook can swivel 360° to allow straps and handles to twist.

LEVER

A lever-style swivel hook has a teardrop shape and spring gate that opens when pushed. The hook can swivel 360° to allow straps and handles to twist.

TRIGGER

A trigger-style swivel hook has a circular shape and is opened by pushing down on a trigger. The hook can swivel 360° to allow straps and handles to pivot.

HARDWARE **57**

Tassel Caps

A tassel cap is a metal cap with a ring or swivel hook attached to the top. Tassel caps are used to cover the tops of tassels, making them easier to attach to bags and accessories.

Zipper & Cord Ends

Zipper and cord ends are metal coverings used to conceal the raw ends of zippers and cords. They are available in a variety of shapes, sizes, and textures.

Evelyn, pattern designed by Sallie Tomato

HANDBAG ZIPPERS

Unfortunately, feelings of fear and hesitation tend to arise when it comes to zippers. However, there is no need to fear or feel discouraged! As with many skills, with a bit of practice you'll soon find that zippers are easy and fun to install. Not only are zippers functional, but they can also be used as decorative accents. Use them for closures, pockets, expandable areas, and more. Understanding the anatomy of a zipper, the types of zippers, and their applications will enable you to select the right zippers and install them into projects with confidence.

Anatomy of a Zipper

A zipper consists of three basic components: teeth, tape, and a slider. The teeth are the individual parts on each side of the zipper that release and engage with each other when the slider passes over them. The teeth allow the zipper to separate into two halves and also to remain securely together. When the two sides of the teeth are secured together, they are called chains. The tape is the material on each side of the zipper that the teeth are attached to. The tape allows the zipper to be attached to apparel, bags, and other goods. The slider joins and separates the teeth to open or close the zipper. A wide range of pull tabs, which are attached to the slider, are available. Circle pulls and donut pulls are perfect for attaching charms or tassels. Some types of zippers also have top and bottom stops.

Sizes

The size of a zipper is determined primarily by the width of the teeth when the zipper is closed. The most common sizes include 3mm, 5mm, 7mm, and 10mm wide. Be sure to use handbag zippers. Including the tape, most handbag zippers are 1¼˝ (3.2mm) wide.

Teeth

METAL

Metal teeth are made from brass, nickel, aluminum, or manganese. Zippers with these types of teeth are used for thick fabrics and items that require frequent opening and closing, such as jackets, uniforms, luggage, and bags.

MOLDED PLASTIC

Molded plastic teeth are made from resin or other plastics. Because they are more lightweight than metal teeth, and will not rust, they are popular for use on accessories; jackets; children's wear; and outdoor, sports, and medical items.

COIL

Coil zipper teeth are made of spiraled plastic such as polyester or nylon. Coil zippers are versatile due to their durability and soft texture. They are commonly used for all sorts of applications such as bags; apparel; furniture; shoes; and outdoor, sports, and medical items.

SPECIALTY TEETH

Specialty teeth are manufactured for specific applications. Some types of specialty teeth include water-repellant, laminated, rubber-coated, crystal, recycled, and unique shapes.

Zipper Types & Applications

CLOSED-END

A closed-end zipper has top and bottom stops that prevent the slider from coming off the tape and the zipper from separating. Closed-end zippers are commonly used for apparel, pockets, upholstery, and other items that don't require the zipper to separate completely.

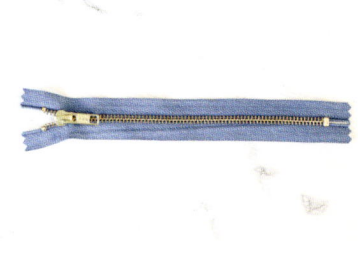

SEPARATING

Separating zippers separate in one direction; or, if they are two-way separating zippers, they can be closed or opened in both directions. Separating zippers are often used for outerwear, sleeping bags, upholstery, and other items that require separating.

DOUBLE-SLIDE ZIPPERS

Double-slide zippers contain two sliders that are positioned head to head. The sliders close the zipper when moved toward each other and open when moved away from each other, allowing the zipper to open from either end. Double-slide zippers are used for bags, luggage, carriers, and outdoor and sports items.

INVISIBLE

Invisible zippers are manufactured so that when the zipper is installed, the teeth cannot be seen from the exterior of the item. This type of zipper is used on items, usually clothing, that require the teeth to be hidden so the zipper doesn't disturb the design. Installing invisible zippers requires special adaptors for the presser foot.

ZIPPER BY THE YARD

Zipper by the yard is a length of zipper that can be cut to yield multiple zippers of a specific length; it can contain a single slider or double sliders. Often, both ends of the zipper by the yard need to be sewn into a seam to prevent the slider from coming off the tape. Parts and tools can be purchased to convert zippers by the yard into closed-end and separating zippers, but the process can be tedious. This type of zipper is used for bags and certain kinds of apparel.

TOOLS & NOTIONS FOR BAG MAKING

Although the pattern design, fabrics, and embellishments may be the most exciting aspects of bag making, using the proper notions and tools is essential for project construction and finishing.

ESSENTIAL BAG MAKING REFERENCE TOOL

Thread

The preferred thread for bag making is 40-weight polyester thread. Polyester thread is stronger than cotton, and this strength is necessary for holding together heavier-weight fabrics and thicker layers. It's durable for both piecing and topstitching.

Needles

Sewing machine needles may all look alike, but in fact the various types are quite different. Selecting the proper needle will allow for ease of sewing through fabrics. Detailed here is a list of the needles most commonly used in bag making, including the best applications for each needle.

DENIM

Denim needles are designed for sewing densely woven fabrics. They have a thick, strong shaft and a very sharp point for consistent stitching. Denim needles sew well through denim, canvas, faux leather, and lightweight leather.

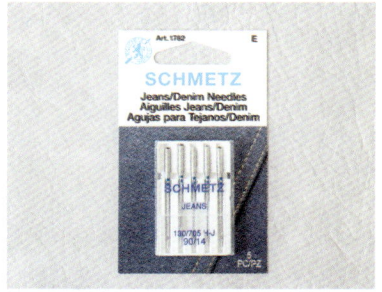

LEATHER

Leather needles are designed for sewing through leather, faux leather, and heavy nonwoven synthetics. This type of needle is designed to pierce the material as the stitch is formed, without tearing the fabric.

TOOLS & NOTIONS FOR BAG MAKING

MICROTEX/SHARP

Microtex needles, also known as sharp needles, have a narrow shaft and a sharp point for finely detailed stitching. This type of needle is ideal for topstitching, quilting, and edgestitching. Microtex needles are designed for microfibers and work well with polyester, silk, faux leather, coated materials, and cork fabric.

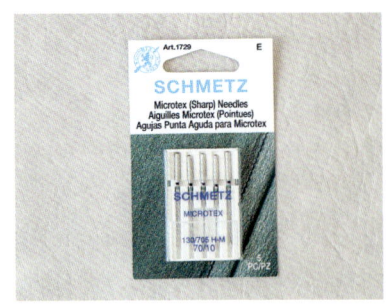

NONSTICK

Nonstick needles are designed for sewing through glue-based or tacky fabrics such as faux leather, flocked fabric, embroidery stabilizers, and other synthetics. The nonstick coating and distinctive design prevent skipped stitches. The point is slightly rounded to provide the ability to sew through most materials.

TOPSTITCH

Topstitch needles are designed for heavy fabric or multiple layers. They have a large shaft, a deep groove, a long eye, and a very sharp point. The large shaft allows for sewing through thicker materials, the deep groove and long eye accommodate heavier threads, and the sharp point allows for straight, precise stitching. For topstitching lightweight fabrics, use a microtex/sharp needle instead.

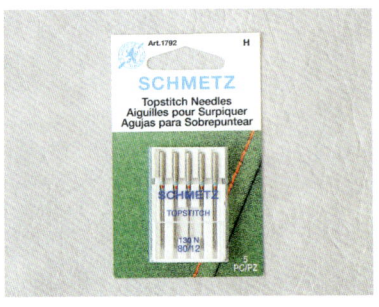

UNIVERSAL

Universal needles are designed for general sewing through both knit and woven fabrics. This type of needle has a slightly rounded ballpoint tip, which is meant to sew through most fabrics. A universal needle is not ideal for sewing through tightly woven fabrics. Instead, use a microtex/sharp needle.

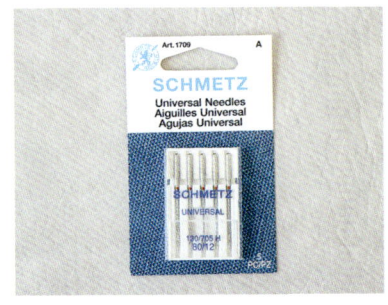

Presser Feet

Take advantage of the vast range of presser feet available on the market. Presser feet can make sewing more pleasurable, offer the ability to add unique details, and yield professional results with ease. This roundup includes common presser feet used in bag making.

ALL-PURPOSE FOOT

The all-purpose foot is designed for general sewing and decorative stitches. This foot is suitable for a variety of techniques and tasks; however, certain fabric types or techniques may be difficult to work with, and another type of foot may be more effective in these cases.

APPLIQUÉ FOOT

The appliqué foot is designed for easy maneuvering around curves and angles when attaching appliqué pieces.

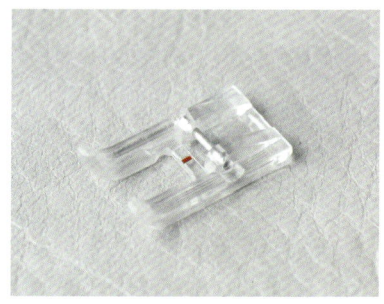

BUTTON SEWING FOOT

The button sewing foot allows buttons, charms, and eyelets to be sewn to projects with a sewing machine rather than hand stitching. To use this foot, set the stitch width to the same width measurement as the gap between the holes on the button, charm, or eyelet.

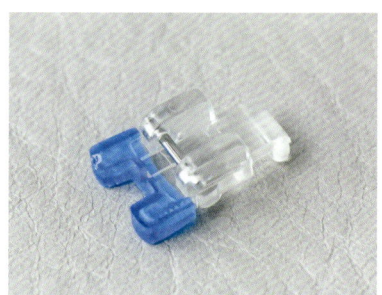

TOOLS & NOTIONS FOR BAG MAKING

BUTTONHOLE FOOT

If your machine can create a one-step buttonhole, you can use a buttonhole foot. The buttonhole foot is designed to stitch custom-sized buttonholes in one simple step.

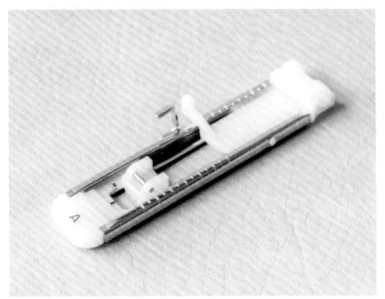

CORDING, PIPING, OR BEADING FEET

Cording, piping, and beading feet are available individually, and some brands are even multipurpose, depending on the shape and size of the foot features. These feet often have one or more grooves on the underside to accurately and evenly feed piping, cording, beading, or even binding.

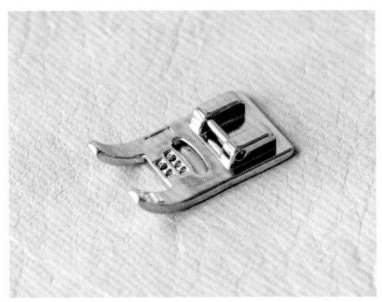

EDGE STITCH FOOT

The edge stitch foot is designed for accurate and even topstitching in the ditch of a seam or along the edge. This foot is also helpful for attaching ribbon or appliqué, or even creating pin tucks.

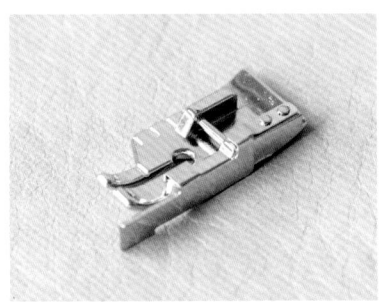

NARROW ZIPPER FOOT

The narrow zipper foot is designed for stitching along the edge of a zipper or along a seam for topstitching, or even for straight-stitch appliqué. It's also handy for sewing on piping and stitching next to hardware for precise installation. The narrow zipper foot provides more visibility than a standard zipper foot.

PINTUCK FOOT

The pintuck foot is used for creating parallel pintucks. The grooves on the underside make the process of creating pintucks quick, easy, and accurate. Pintucks are used to decorate clothing, household items, and bags.

ROLLER FOOT

The roller foot has rollers at the front and back that help to feed pieces with uneven levels, or fabrics that are difficult to sew over, such as faux leather, velvet, or vinyl. This foot also helps improve stitch quality.

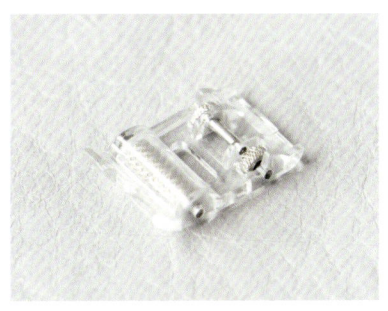

RUFFLER FOOT

The ruffler foot is designed to enable the creation of evenly spaced and accurate gathers or ruffles. Adjust the stitch length based on the desired fullness of the gathers. This foot can save time and creates a uniform finish for clothing, home decor, and bags.

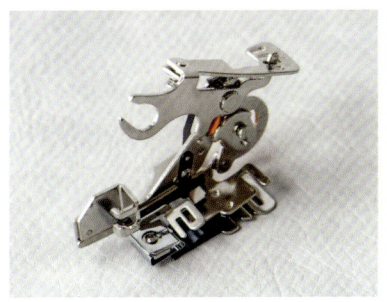

STRAIGHT STITCH FOOT

The straight stitch foot has a single hole and a narrow view of the fabric, so the foot can apply more pressure to the feed dogs. This helps hold the fabric in place while stitching, for a consistent straight stitch.

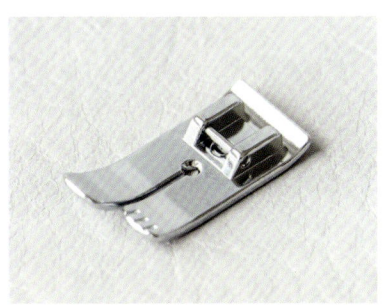

TEFLON FOOT

The Teflon foot is essential for bag making, since it's designed for sewing tacky fabrics such as faux leather, vinyl, laminated cotton, and leather. The foot has a nonstick coating that allows fabrics to glide under it easily.

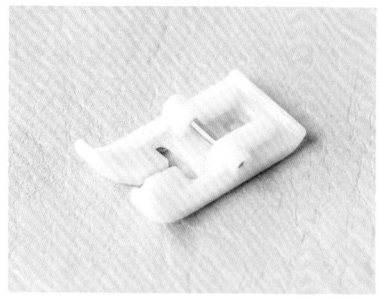

TEFLON ZIPPER FOOT

The Teflon zipper foot is a zipper foot with a Teflon coating to make inserting and topstitching zippers a breeze. It's also useful for close topstitching and edgestitching of difficult-to-feed fabrics such as faux leather, vinyl, laminated cotton, and leather.

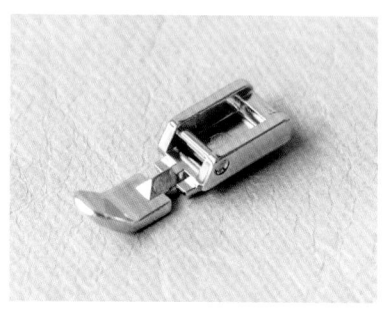

WALKING FOOT

The walking foot, also known as the even-feed foot, is designed to feed layers of fabric through the machine evenly and at a consistent rate. Use the walking foot for quilting or sewing bags, patchwork, and even clothing.

ZIPPER FOOT

The zipper foot is used for inserting and topstitching zippers, trim, piping, and other embellishments on bags, home decor, and apparel. Most zipper feet are adjustable to correspond with the position of the zipper tape.

Marking Tools

Having a variety of marking tools on hand is crucial when you are working with different materials. The proper marking tool will depend on the type and color of the fabric. Whenever possible, always mark on the wrong side of the fabric so the markings won't be visible on the finished project. This section provides a list of helpful marking tools for bag making.

AIR-ERASABLE

Air-erasable marking tools are convenient and leave no trace, as the ink disappears after a few hours or days, depending on the type.

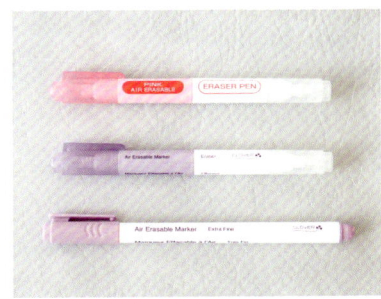

CHALK

Chalk is easy to see on fabrics and will leave a mark on synthetic fabrics, where ink may not. Options for chalk include tailor's chalk, chalk wheels, and chalk pencils, all available in a variety of colors to appear on different fabrics.

IRON-AWAY

Iron-away pens and markers leave an easy-to-see mark that can be quickly removed. Simply touch the mark with the hot plate of your iron or with steam, and the marking will disappear.

RUB-AWAY

Rub-away pens leave a visible mark that easily rubs off with pressure from your finger or the opposite end of the pen.

WASH-AWAY

The markings made by wash-away pens and markers are easy to see and are quickly removed with a damp cloth or sponge. Make sure water will not damage your fabric before using a wash-away pen.

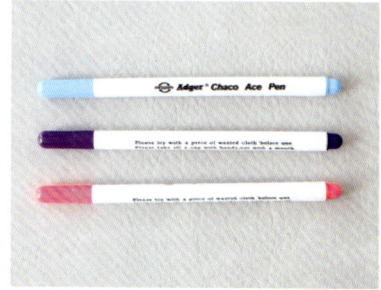

Adhesives

Adhesives, such as glues and tapes, are especially handy for heavier-weight fabrics and synthetic materials. Various products are available to either temporarily or permanently hold areas that might not be able to fit under your sewing machine foot, or to reinforce straps and seams and secure hardware.

GLUES

Glue is used to either temporarily or permanently hold fabrics together and secure hardware and embellishments in place. Some options include hot glue, industrial-strength glue, basting spray, leather glue or cement, and craft glue.

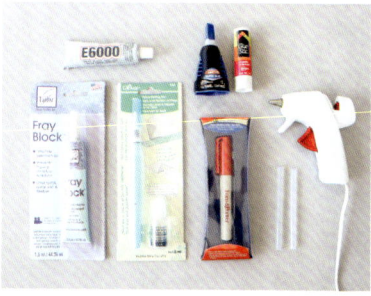

TAPES

Tape can be handy for securing areas that are difficult to hold together with pins or sewing clips, holding hardware in place, and even repairing bags. Options include double-sided basting tape, paper tape, and leather repair tape.

Pressing Tools

It's the pattern you use that determines the shape of your bag, but it's the pressing and finishing that add structure and additional form. Pressing tools are a bag maker's best-kept secret when it comes to achieving professional results. Make sure to have these tools on hand, as you may need them for a variety of applications.

IRON

An iron is essential for removing creases and pressing folds and seams for all types of sewing. A steam iron will help eliminate wrinkles on bags that contain foam interfacing or cork. A small travel-sized iron is great for quick pressing next to your sewing machine.

HERA MARKER & CREASER

A Hera Marker marks and makes creases that can be seen on both sides of the fabric, without leaving any residue, unlike other marking tools. This tool is especially useful for marking waxed canvas. Hera Markers have a curved end, which can also be used for smoothing out seams or corners.

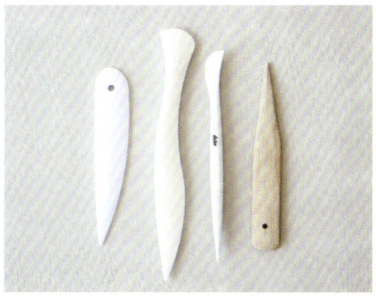

SEAM ROLLER

A seam roller is used for quick and convenient pressing of seams and edges. The roller will not distort the fabric as you apply pressure and push the tool along the seam or edge.

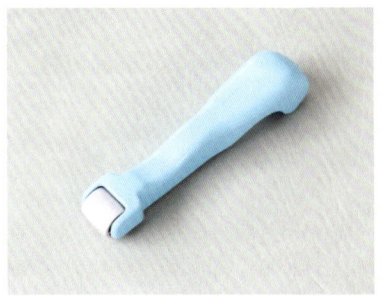

HOT RULER

A hot ruler, or hot hemmer, can be used to measure, mark, and press straight or curved hems. The ruler is made from heat-resistant material, allowing you to iron directly on the ruler. This tool allows for precise measuring and pressing. In bag making, it's useful for pressing pocket and flap edges.

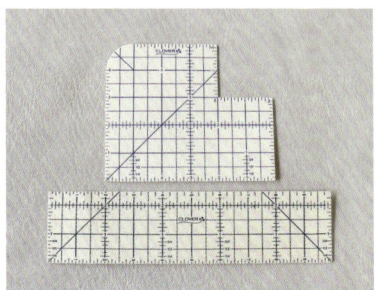

Cutting Tools

Often, cutting can be a long, tedious part of the process of preparing your fabrics for sewing. It's important to use tools that are sharp and comfortable to grip to prevent soreness and allow for quick, accurate cutting.

ROTARY CUTTER & MAT

A rotary cutter and cutting mat are convenient tools for making quick and accurate straight cuts. A rotary cutter has a sharp circular blade. Common blade sizes for bag making include 28mm for more delicate fabrics and 45mm for medium- to heavyweight fabrics.

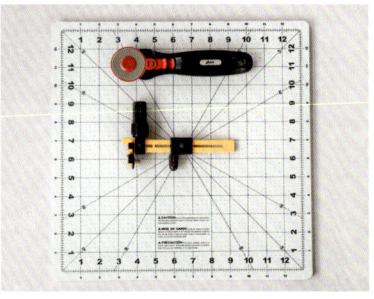

A rotary cutter requires a cutting mat as a safe cutting surface. The mat also prevents the blade from getting dull. Cutting mats are made from a durable material such as rubber, vinyl, or polypropylene.

SCISSORS

A sharp pair of fabric scissors is essential for bag making, as you frequently need to cut through multiple layers of fabric and interfacing, as well as thicker materials. A quality pair of thread snips is handy for trimming thread tails for professional final results.

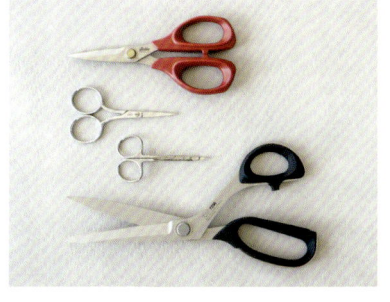

Also, pinking shears are helpful for clipping curves and reducing bulk.

Hardware Tools

Don't be intimidated to use tools, because they exist to help you! Hardware tools of the trade are helpful to aid in construction quality and accuracy. Most projects will need only common tools such as a seam ripper and screwdriver. However, some hardware requires special tools for installation. This list of basic tools is a great starting point for beginners.

AWLS

Awls are useful for marking, punching, and opening holes. They can also be used to help feed fabric through a sewing machine. Awls are designed for detail work such as pulling out corners, untying threads, and widening spaces.

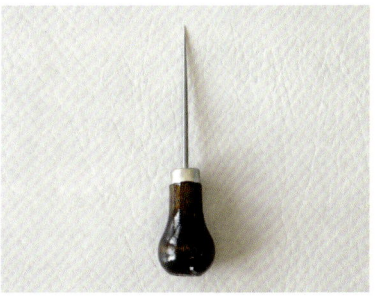

HAMMERS & MALLETS

Hammers work well for compressing bulk in seams, installing select hardware, and forming leather. Mallets can be used with hole cutters, setting tools, and more.

HOLE CUTTERS & PUNCHES

Use hole cutters and punches to cut accurate holes and slits for hardware installation, ribbons, and lace. Simply position the cutter over your project and strike the top with a mallet, or squeeze the handles together, to cut through thicker fabrics and multiple layers.

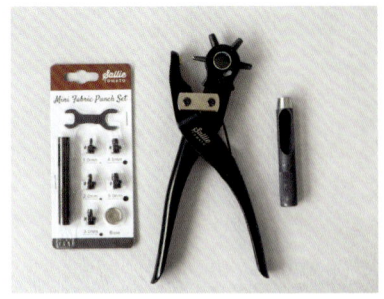

PLIERS

Pliers are especially useful for holding objects firmly, compressing materials, and bending the prongs of hardware. Use the jaws to grip small screws or delicate embellishments. Rubber-coated pliers can be used for clamping hardware without scratching the finish.

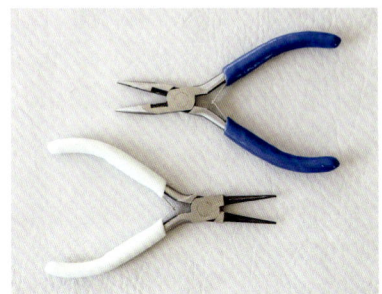

RIVET TOOLS

Rivets can be quickly installed with a set of rivet tools, which includes a setter and an anvil. Using the correct size of setting tool is essential for proper installation and a strong bond connection between parts. To determine the correct size, choose tools based on the cap width.

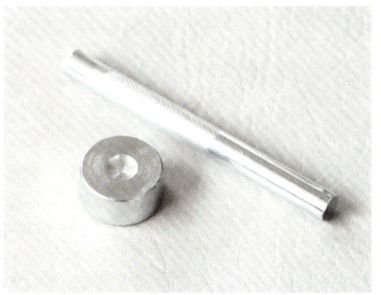

ROTARY PUNCHES

A rotary punch will accurately cut holes through multiple layers of material. Punch holes for lacings, stitching, rivets, screws, bag feet, or other hardware. The punch features a strong steel body, a brass anvil, and a locking wheel with varying tube sizes. Simply set the punch to the desired tube size and squeeze the handle to cut a hole.

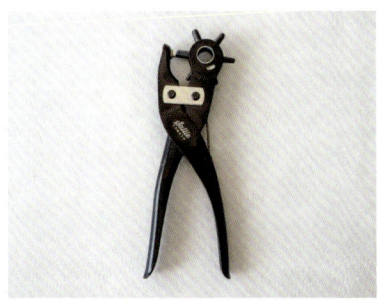

SCREWDRIVERS

Screwdrivers are essential for select types of hardware such as locks, strap connectors, zipper ends, strap ends, tassel caps, and Chicago screws. Most screw-in hardware requires a Phillips screwdriver, but some brands might require a flat-head screwdriver. The most common sizes to use for purse hardware are sizes #0 and #1.

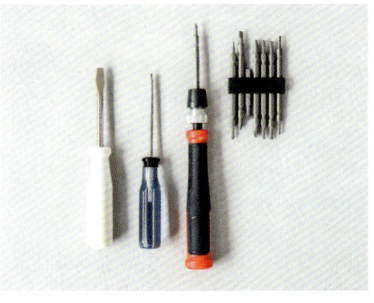

SEAM RIPPERS

A sharp seam ripper is an essential tool for more than just removing stitches. It can also be used for cutting slits for installing hardware with prongs and for aiding in zipper installation or creating other placement openings and markings.

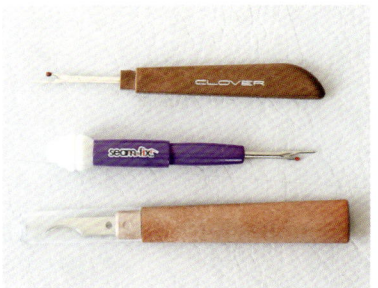

SNAP FASTENER TOOLS

Snap fastener tools are used for setting plastic or metal snaps. Using the correct size and type of snap setting tool is essential for proper installation and a strong connection between parts.

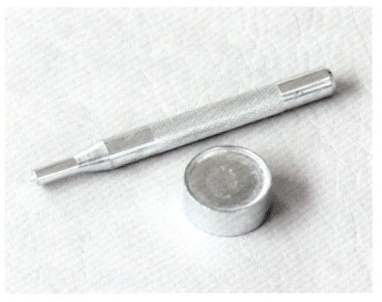

Other Handy Items

Sewing notions are small tools and accessories used to complete sewing projects. This list of other handy notions includes items that are helpful to have on hand but that are not necessary for all projects. Understanding the notions available on the market will help you best select the ones you need for your project.

BIAS TAPE

Bias tape is a narrow, continuous strip of fabric that has been cut on the bias of the fabric and folded and pressed. Since the strip fibers are at a 45° angle, the fabric has more stretch. Bias tape is commonly used to cover and finish off the raw edges of apparel, bags, quilts, and home decor projects.

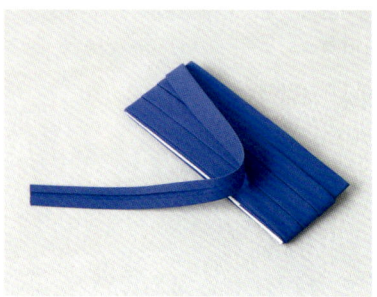

CREASING & TURNING TOOLS

Creasing and turning tools can help you push out corners and tight spaces, smooth curved edges, and press and crease fabric. These multipurpose tools are available in a variety of shapes and sizes.

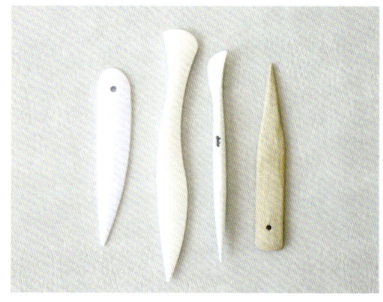

EDGE PAINT

Edge paint is used for coating and sealing the edges of leather and other fabrics on straps, handles, and projects with exposed raw edges. Most edge paints are rubberized or are enamel to withstand use. Edge paint can also improve the final appearance of the bag.

HOOK-AND-LOOP TAPE

Hook-and-loop tape is used for fastening pockets, flaps, and other components on bags, apparel, and home decor projects. One side of the tape has tiny hooks and the other side has loops. The hook side clings to the loop side, and the two sides are easily pressed together or pulled apart. Sew-in and adhesive options are available.

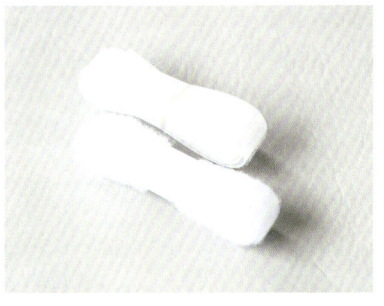

MAGNETS

Strong magnets are useful in bag making, as well as in English paper piecing, apparel sewing, and machine embroidery. Use magnets to hold together pieces that cannot be pinned or held with sewing clips. They're ideal for hard-to-reach places and thick fabrics that you can't puncture with pins.

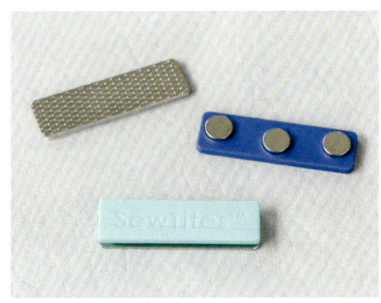

PINS

Pins are used to temporarily hold layers of fabric together. Glass-head or heat-resistant pins are useful for areas that need to be held together during ironing. In bag making, use pins to hold pockets, zippers, flaps, and other areas in place.

RULERS

Rulers are necessary for measuring and cutting pieces accurately. A variety of sizes and shapes are useful for different purposes. Longer cuts such as straps, handles, and gussets are quickly cut with a long quilting ruler. Smaller rulers are handy for convenient measuring next to your sewing machine; marking seam allowances; measuring hardware placement; and cutting smaller or more delicate pieces such as strap connectors, zipper tabs, and tassel fringe.

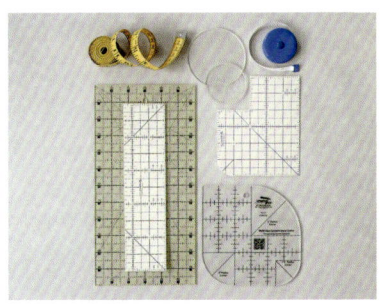

SEAM GUIDE

A magnetic seam guide helps maintain a consistent seam allowance.

SEWING CLIPS

Sewing clips are essential for holding together thicker layers, heavyweight fabrics, or fabrics with a high pile. They are a great alternative to pins since they don't puncture or distort fabrics. Sewing clips are easy to hold, open, and close, and they won't prick your fingers or bend.

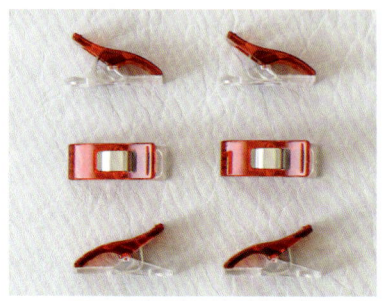

STILETTO

A stiletto has a pointed end that is used to help guide fabric and prevent it from shifting during sewing. It's ideal for stitching narrow seams, embellishments, and hard-to-hold areas.

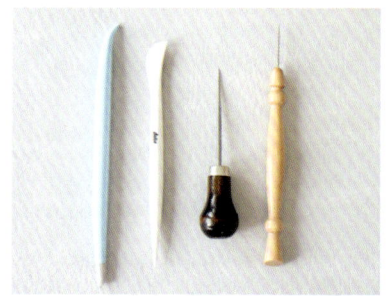

WEBBING

Webbing is a woven material with finished edges made from cotton, nylon, polyester, or polypropylene. Webbing is a quick option for making durable straps, handles, or belts. It's also used in load-bearing applications such as items for pets; sporting goods; and outdoor, nautical, and apparel items. The cut ends are raw and will need to be finished or sewn into a seam.

STRUCTURE & SHAPING

Everyone wants to know the secrets to structuring and shaping bags for the most professional results. There are a variety of techniques that can be used to add structure and shape, including interfacing, stabilizing, reducing bulk, and even features within the pattern design itself. This chapter dives into popular techniques, tips, and strategies for structuring and shaping bags, all of which can be achieved using a home sewing machine and ordinary notions.

Interfacing, Stabilizing & Reducing Bulk

Gone are the days of using only quilt batting for stabilizing bags. Thankfully, today's sewing products have advanced, and pattern designers have developed innovative techniques from studying how large manufacturers produce ready-made bags and applying their secrets to home sewing. Generally, a simple formula for structuring bags is to apply interfacing to the exterior and interior, add another interfacing between the exterior and interior, and, lastly, reduce bulk to create a sturdy bag. Of course, depending on the design and characteristics of the bag—taking into account its fabric, shape, pockets, closures, straps, and handles—more or maybe less interfacing and/or support materials may be needed. Use this basic formula as a guide when planning out your projects.

Start by selecting an interfacing that's appropriate for the main type of fabric you're using. For guidance on selecting interfacing, refer to Fabrics & Interfacing (page 25). The best practice for a crisp, stable interior and pockets is to also interface the lining fabric. Additional interfacing may need to be added to areas with heavy use, such as pockets, hardware, bottoms, gussets, straps, and handles. Less interfacing may be needed in thicker areas such as seams with multiple layers of fabric, corners, flap edges, gathered or pleated features, drawstrings, and other closures.

Next, select an interfacing to use between the exterior and interior layers to add body and stability. Tried-and-true options include fleece, batting, and foam interfacing. The choice ultimately depends on the fabrics used and the desired form of the bag. The final piece of the formula is to reduce bulk. One of the simplest ways to reduce bulk is to avoid interfacing in the seam allowance. Either cut the interfacing smaller, omitting the seam allowance, or trim the interfacing away from the seam allowance after you complete the stitching. Another tip to compress bulky seams is to hammer the seam with a mallet. The fabrics will be temporarily flattened for easier stitching and crisp edges. Bulky seams can further be compressed by stitching a second line ⅛" (3mm) or ¼" (6mm) from the first stitch line. The second line of stitching will also take away some of the stress on the first seam, making the seam even more stable.

Lastly, trim all seam allowances after stitching. For bag construction, it's important to have a wider seam allowance, such as ⅜" (1cm) or ½" (12mm) wide, to catch all the layers and thicker fabrics; however, to reduce bulk after sewing, the seam allowances can be trimmed back to ⅛" (3mm) or ¼" (6mm) wide, depending on the fabric and area of the bag.

> **TIP** · *To add stability to bags, use support materials such as bag bases, metal frames, or piping and cording. For detailed explanations and examples of how to use support materials, refer to Fabrics & Interfacing (page 25). These materials are often applied in more advanced designs and bag making techniques; however, incorporating them into simpler projects is still very achievable.*

Adding Depth & Shape

SEW A BOXED BOTTOM

A boxed bottom is a flat bottom in the shape of a rectangle. This style is preferred for bags that hold wider things. Bags with a boxed bottom can usually stand upright on their own, depending on the depth of the bottom. Make the boxed bottom with the exterior fabric and then repeat with the lining fabric.

Beginner Tote Project from *Making Bags* by Jessica Barrera

1. With the right sides together, align the side seam with the bottom seam.

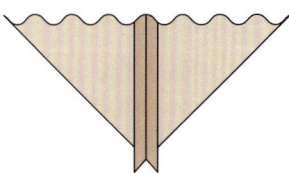

2. Measure and mark a line equal to half the depth of the bag perpendicular to the seams.

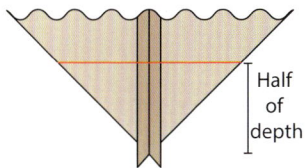

Half of depth

3. Stitch on the line; then trim away the excess corner fabric, leaving a ¼″ (6mm) wide seam allowance.

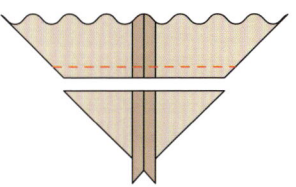

STRUCTURE & SHAPING 83

Alternative Method

An alternative method for making a boxed bottom is to first cut a square out of each corner of the bottom exterior or lining fabric, with the square measuring half the depth of your bag.

Then, with the right sides together, match the side seam with the bottom seam, align the raw edges at each corner, and sew ¼˝ (6mm) from the raw edges.

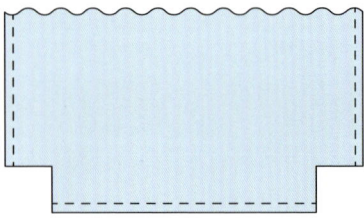

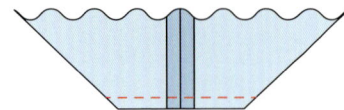

DARTS

A dart is a folded area of fabric leading to a point that adds dimension and shape to the bottom of bags. This style is preferred for smaller bags that are carried across the body or over the shoulder and don't need a lot of depth. Create darts on both the exterior and lining fabrics so the shapes will match.

Scarlett, pattern by Sallie Tomato

1. Cut a narrow triangle from each corner of the bottom of the bag, with the point at a 45° angle toward the center.

2. Then, with the right sides together, align the raw edges of the dart and sew ¼˝ (6mm) from the raw edges, up to the fold.

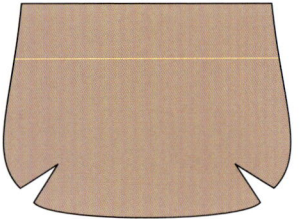

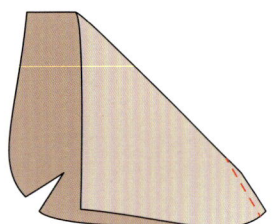

GUSSETS

Another method to add depth and shape is to use a gusset. A gusset is a strip of fabric that joins the front and back of the bag. Gussets can be added to the bottom base only, to the sides, or as a full continuous piece around the sides and base. Generally, gussets follow the shape of the front and back of the bag,

Holly, pattern by Sallie Tomato, showing full gusset

meaning they can be attached to corners as well as curves. Also, gussets can have edges that are straight, tapered, or shaped to add additional structure or form to the bag. This style is preferred for bags that hold wide things and, usually, for bags that include a variety of pockets and organizer elements.

SEWING CURVES

Curves can be added not only to the exterior edges of the bag but also to the edges of pockets, strap ends, flaps, gussets, and other accents. Curves can be incorporated into nearly any style of bag in a range of sizes and degrees of complexity. Curved edges can often be intimidating to sew; however, you can achieve good results if you simply take your time and stop to pivot the presser foot often to maintain an even seam allowance width. Some tips for sewing successful curves:

- Mark the seam allowance along the curved edges before sewing.
- Use a shorter stitch length to achieve a smoother stitch line.
- After sewing, cut small notches or slits along the curve to remove bulk in the seam before turning the piece right side out.

STRUCTURE & SHAPING

PART THREE
Bag Making Skills

CLOSURES, POCKETS, STRAPS & HANDLES

Learning the basic construction methods for common closures, pockets, straps, and handles will help build your confidence in bag making. However, keep in mind that once you know the basic process of how to assemble these bag features, you'll need to adapt the dimensions or technique for your specific project. This chapter is a roundup of basic tutorials on features commonly used in bag making, including closures, essential pockets, and straps and handles.

Closures

DRAWSTRING

1. Sew the entire bag, attaching the exterior and interior, along with all other components.

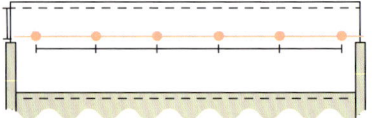

2. To create the drawstring closure, mark equally spaced placement locations for an even number of grommets, on both the front and back. Consider the size of the grommets when marking the placement distance from the top edge.

3. Use a grommet hole cutter or scissors to cut holes the appropriate size for the grommets. The holes should be slightly larger than the inner diameter of the grommets.

4. Install a grommet over each hole.

5. Create a drawstring using your desired method. The width of the drawstring should be ⅛˝ to ¼˝ (3 to 6mm) less than the inner diameter of the grommets. The length should generally be the circumference measurement of the bag plus an extra 6˝ (15.2cm).

6. Create a drawstring tab from faux leather or cork fabric. Cut a piece 1˝ (2.5cm) high by double the width of the drawstring, plus 1˝ (2.5cm). With the right sides together, fold the tab in half, aligning the side edges, and sew ¼˝ (6mm) from each side. Turn the tab right side out. Center the seam on one side of the tab. Topstitch ¼″ (6mm) from each side of the seam.

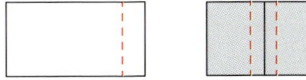

7. Thread the drawstring through one of the middle grommets on the front of your bag. Continue weaving the same end of the drawstring through all the grommets, moving alternately from the inside to the outside of the bag.

The end of the drawstring should come out through the other middle grommet on the front.

8. Thread each end of the drawstring through the tab. Knot the ends of the drawstring either separately or together; otherwise, finish off the ends of the drawstring with tassel caps or cord ends.

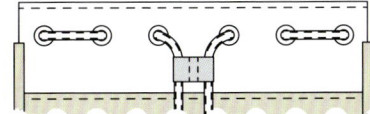

MAGNETIC SNAP

For instructions on how to install a magnetic snap closure with prongs, refer to Installing Magnetic Snaps (page 50).

PURSE FRAME

Before constructing the bag, shape the upper edge to fit the purse frame, allowing for the upper edge and side seam allowances. After constructing the bag, coat the inner channel of one side of the purse frame with a generous amount of permanent glue from edge to edge. Center and push the upper edge of

Silvia, pattern designed by Sallie Tomato

the bag into the channel. A flat-head screwdriver can help you push the fabric further into the channel, so the upper edge is pushed tight against the hardware. For additional reinforcement, segments of twine can be pushed into the channel. Attach large binder clips or clothespins over the upper edge and frame to hold the bag edge in place while the glue dries. Once the glue has dried, repeat the same process to insert the opposite edge of the bag into the other half of the purse frame. Use rubber-coated pliers, or standard pliers with a scrap of batting over the jaws, to squeeze the corners and edges of the purse frame together slightly for further reinforcement.

CLOSURES, POCKETS, STRAPS & HANDLES

TOP ZIPPER
Install Zipper with Tabs

Beginner Tote Project from *Making Bags* by Jessica Barrera

1. With the wrong sides together, fold each main fabric zipper tab piece in half.

2. Slide a tab over each end of the zipper, so the ends of the zipper are tucked inside the tabs. Each end of the zipper should be pushed tight against the fold of the tab. Use basting tape or sewing clips to hold the tabs in place.

3. Topstitch the tabs to the zipper ⅛˝ (3mm) from the raw edges.

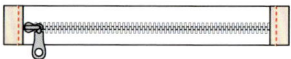

4. With the right sides together, center the zipper along the top edge of the main fabric front panel. Use a zipper foot or narrow foot to baste the zipper in place with a ¼˝ (6mm) seam allowance. Make sure the zipper pull is out of the way as you sew.

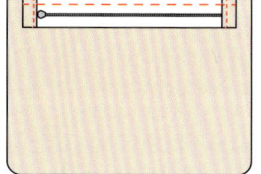

5. With the right sides together, layer the lining front panel over the main fabric front panel and zipper, aligning all the edges. Sew together along the top edge with a ⅜˝ (1cm) seam allowance, moving the zipper pull out of the way as needed.

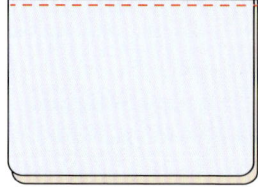

6. Press the seam open with your finger or a seam roller. Topstitch ⅛˝ (3mm) from each side of the seam, moving the zipper out of the way.

7. With the right sides together, center and baste the zipper along the top edge of the main fabric back panel. Layer the lining back panel right sides together with the lining front panel and zipper, aligning the top and side edges. Sew together along the top edge with a ⅜˝ (1cm) seam allowance.

8. Press the seam open with your finger or a seam roller. Topstitch ⅛˝ (3mm) from each side of the seam, moving the zipper out of the way.

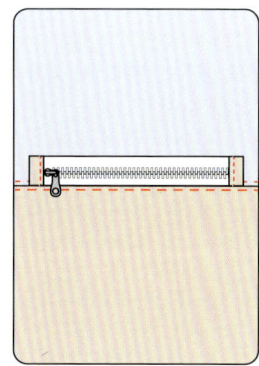

Install Zipper Without Tabs

1. Attach a zipper end to the closed end of the zipper, according to the manufacturer's instructions.

2. At the open end of the zipper, turn each end of the zipper tape under at a right angle and stitch in place.

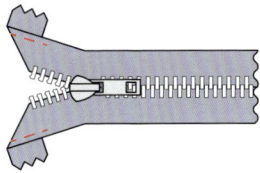

3. Open the zipper completely. With the right sides together, position one side of the zipper along the top raw edge of the exterior. The folded end of the zipper should be ¼" (6mm) from the side seam. Position the opposite end of the zipper away from the top edge, 1½" (3.8cm) from the side seam. The seam should taper off the zipper tape ½" (12mm) from the side seam. Sew the zipper in place with a ¼" (6mm) seam allowance. Make sure to backstitch over each end.

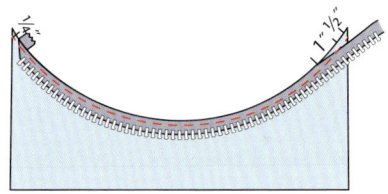

4. Repeat Step 3 to attach the remaining side of the zipper to the opposite side of the exterior. After sewing, test your zipper to make sure it opens and closes evenly. Open the zipper completely and turn the exterior wrong side out.

Essential Pockets

SLIP POCKET

The cut size of the pocket is determined by the size and shape of the bag. Be sure to consider how the base and sides of the bag will form after assembly.

1. Cut 2 same-size pieces, including ¼" (6mm) seam allowances. With right sides together, pin and sew the edges together with a ¼" (6mm) seam allowance, leaving an opening along the bottom edge.

2. Trim the seam allowance at the corners, but do not cut through the stitching. Turn the pocket right side out. Turn the seam allowance at the opening to the wrong side, creating an even edge along the bottom. Press; then topstitch ⅛" (3mm) from the top edge.

CLOSURES, POCKETS, STRAPS & HANDLES

3. With the right sides up, position the slip pocket according to the pattern or project instructions, or as desired. Pin in place. Topstitch ⅛" (3mm) from the side and bottom edges.

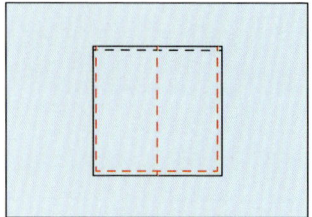

Slip Pocket Variations

Depending on the location of the slip pocket and the material used, you may want to consider adding a hardware closure, such as a magnetic snap, lock, or snap fastener (see Locks & Closures, page 47).

> **TIP** · *For additional reinforcement, topstitch a second line ¼" (6mm) from the side and bottom edges. Depending on the size of the slip pocket, you may want to stitch one or more vertical lines through the pocket to divide it into compartments.*

ZIPPER POCKET

Determine the cut length and width of the zipper pocket by referring to the size of the bag. Be sure to consider how the base and sides of the bag will form after assembly. Zipper pockets can be added to the exterior of a bag as well as to the lining.

1. Cut 2 same-size pieces, including ¼" (6mm) seam allowances on the top and sides and a ½" (12mm) seam allowance on the bottom edge. Select a zipper length that is the same measurement as the pocket width. Press the bottom edge of each pocket piece ½" (12mm) to the wrong side.

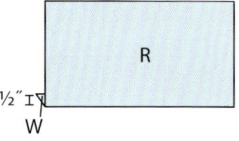

2. Measure and mark the zipper placement box. On the wrong side of a pocket piece, mark a horizontal line ¾" (19mm) down from the top edge. Mark a second horizontal line ½" (12mm) below the first line. Mark a vertical line ¾" (19mm) in from each side.

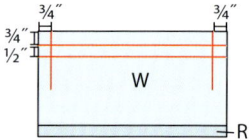

3. With the right sides together, position the marked pocket piece on the bag panel according to the pattern or project instructions, or as desired. Pin in place. Sew along the lines of the zipper placement box, pivoting at each corner.

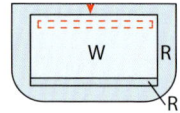

4. Use small scissors or a seam ripper to carefully cut a horizontal line through the center of the stitched placement box, stopping about ½" (12mm) from each end. Cut diagonally toward the stitched corners at each end. Make sure to cut through all the layers, but do not cut through the stitching.

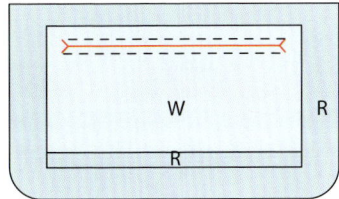

5. Push the pocket piece through the cut opening to the wrong side and place the fabrics wrong sides together. Press in place from both sides.

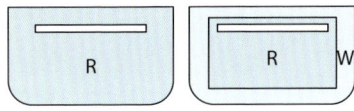

6. On the wrong side of the bag panel, center the zipper right side down over the placement opening. The right side of the zipper should show through the opening on the right side of the bag panel. Use basting tape or glue to hold the zipper in place.

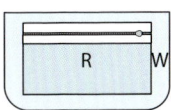

7. On the right side of the bag panel, topstitch ⅛" (3mm) from the zipper placement opening using a zipper foot or narrow presser foot.

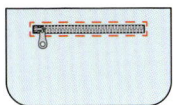

8. On the wrong side of the bag panel, align all the edges of the remaining pocket piece, right sides together, with the attached pocket piece. Pin only the pocket pieces together. Fold the bag panel away from the pinned top edge of the pocket. Sew along the top edge with a ⅝" (16mm) seam allowance.

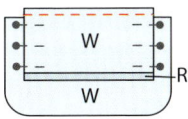

9. Fold the bag panel away from the pinned sides of the pocket. Sew along each side edge with a ¼" (6mm) seam allowance.

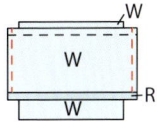

10. Unfold the bag panel and press away any creases. Unzip the zipper completely to prepare the bag for turning after assembly. Continue with the assembly of the bag. Once the bag is assembled, it can be turned right side out through the zipper pocket opening. After turning, stitch the opening in the pocket closed with an ⅛" (3mm) seam allowance.

TIP · *If you do not turn the bag right side out through the zipper pocket opening, the opening in the pocket can be stitched closed at any stage.*

Zipper Pocket Variations

Depending on the location and material of the zipper pocket, you may want to consider adding a cover to conceal the zipper or adding an accent to highlight the zipper.

Straps & Handles

ADJUSTABLE STRAP

1. Determine the finished width of the strap. Use 1 slider buckle and 2 swivel hooks that accommodate the same width as the strap.

2. For webbing, cut 1 piece 50˝ (127cm) long. To prevent the raw ends from unraveling, melt the raw ends by lightly touching them

with a lighter. If you're not comfortable melting the raw ends, sew over the ends several times using a wide zigzag stitch. Proceed to Step 7.

3. For cork or faux leather, cut 2 pieces 25˝ (64cm) long by double the finished width.

4. Join the strap pieces by placing the short ends right sides together, perpendicular to each other, overlapping the ends. Sew a diagonal seam from corner to corner.

5. Trim the excess seam allowance to ¼˝ (6mm) wide. Press the seam open. Topstitch ⅛˝ (3mm) from each side of the seam.

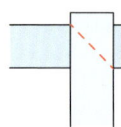
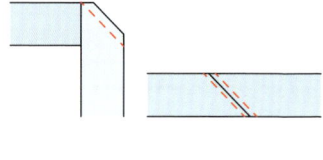

6. With the wrong sides together, fold the strap in half lengthwise. Topstitch ⅛˝ (3mm) from each long edge.

7. Thread an end of the strap over the center bar of a slider buckle. Fold the end of the strap under about 1˝ (2.5cm) and topstitch the end to the strap.

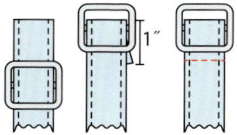

2. Mark the placement of the handles on the right side of the main fabric front and back panels.

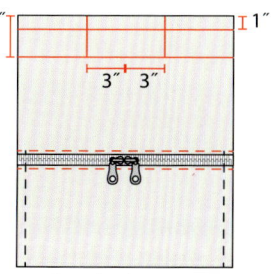

Sample placement

8. Thread the opposite end through a swivel hook, and then thread the end over the center bar of the slider buckle.

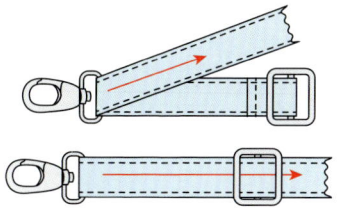

3. Adhere basting tape to 2˝ (5.1cm) of each end of 1 handle piece on the wrong side. With the right sides facing up, position the handle ends inside the markings on the main fabric front. Topstitch each end of the handle in place ⅛˝ (3mm) from the edges, up to the marked 1˝ (2.5cm) line, and stitch across.

9. To complete the strap, thread the end through the remaining swivel hook. Fold the end of the strap under about 1˝ (2.5cm) and topstitch the end to the strap.

BASIC SHOULDER STRAP & HANDLES

Convert any handles into shoulder straps by simply cutting them longer.

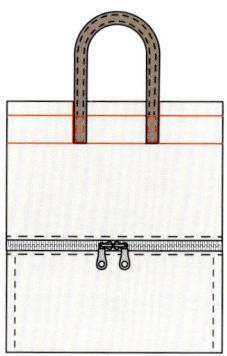

1. With the wrong sides together, fold each handle piece in half lengthwise. Topstitch ⅛˝ (3mm) from each long side.

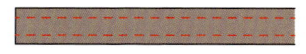

4. Repeat Step 3 to attach the remaining handle to the main fabric back. Remove the marks.

5. If desired, install a small rivet centered ½˝ (12mm) up from each end of the handles (see Installing Rivets, page 54).

TIP · *If desired, cut each of the ends to be pointed or rounded to your liking.*

CLOSURES, POCKETS, STRAPS & HANDLES

Strap Connectors

1. With the wrong sides together, fold each long edge of each strap connector to the center. Topstitch ¼˝ (6mm) from each long edge of each strap connector.

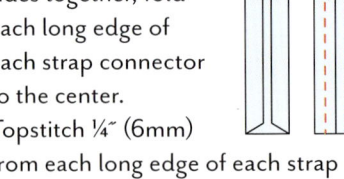

2. Slide an O-ring over the end of each strap connector. Fold the raw ends of each strap connector so they meet in the middle, which will be the underside, encasing the O-ring.

3. Pin the raw ends in place. With the right sides up, center a strap connector over each side seam of the assembled exterior, so the top fold is 1˝ (2.5cm) down from the top edge and the O-ring is at the top. Use pins or basting tape to hold each strap connector in place. Use a zipper foot or narrow foot to topstitch each strap connector along the hardware, and then pivot to sew ⅛˝ (3mm) from the remaining edges.

4. Thread an end of the shoulder strap through an O-ring on the bag from the outside toward the inside. Fold under the end of the shoulder strap 1˝ (25mm). Topstitch ⅛˝ (3mm) and ¼˝ (6mm) from the raw end. Repeat to attach the opposite end of the shoulder strap to the remaining O-ring.

WRISTLET STRAP

1. The most versatile and durable way to make and attach a wristlet strap is by using key fob hardware and cork fabric or faux leather. Cut 1 piece 2˝ × 12˝ (5 × 30.5cm) for the strap. With the wrong sides together, fold the strap in half lengthwise. Topstitch ⅛˝ (3mm) from each long edge.

2. Fold the strap in half, matching the short ends. Insert the short ends into the key fob hardware. Clamp the hardware over the strap ends.

TIP • Use rubber-coated pliers to clamp the hardware to prevent it from being scratched. If you don't have rubber-coated pliers, cover the key fob with a scrap of batting or foam before clamping it together.

Index

A
accordion bags, 12
adhesives, 72–73

B
backpacks, 12
bag care, 22–24
bag types, 12–21
baguettes, 13
barrel bags, 13
beginner bags, 7
bowling bags, 13
boxed bottoms, 83–84
bracelet bags, 14
briefcase bags, 18
bucket bags, 14
buckles, 42–43

C
camera bags, 14
canteen bags, 15
caring for bags, 22–24
cleaning and conditioning bags, 22–23
closures, 11, 86–89
clutches, 15
cosmetics bags, 16
crossbody bags, 15
cutting tools, 74–75

D
daypacks, 12
diaper bags, 16
doctor's bags, 16
Dopp kits, 16
drawstring bags, 17
drawstring closure, 86–87
duffle bags, 17

F
fabrics, 25
canvas, 26
cork, 26
cotton, 27
denim, 27
Essex linen, 28
faux fur, 29
faux leather, 28
flannel, 29
fur, 29
Kraft-tex, 30
laminated cotton, 30
leather, 7, 30
mesh, 31
microsuede, 32
oilcloth, 31
ripstop, 33
sequins, 32
suede, 32
velvet/velveteen, 33
vinyl, 34
waxed canvas, 34
frames, 45

H
handbags, 17
handles & straps, 11, 56, 92–94
hardware, 40
bag feet, 41
buckles, 42–43
chain, 44
Chicago screws, 54
conchos, 44
cord ends, 58
cord locks, 44
eyelets, 46
frames, 45
grommets, 46
handles, metal, 51
hanging finish, 40
key fobs, 46
labels, 46
locks & closures, 47–50
magnetic snaps, 50–51
rings, 51–53
rivets, 54
rolling finish, 40
snap fasteners, 55
spots, 56
strap hardware, 56
stud buttons, 57
swivel hooks, 57
tassel caps, 58
zipper ends, 58
hobo bags, 18

I–L
insulated bags, 18
interfacing, 25, 35–38
laptop bags, 18
locks & closures, 47–49, 86–89

M
magnetic snaps, 50–51, 87
marking tools, 71–72
messenger bags, 19

N
needles, 65–66
notions
bias tape, 78
creasing tools, 78
edge paint, 78
hook-and-loop tape, 79
magnets, 79
pins, 79
rulers, 79
seam guide, 80
sewing clips, 80
stiletto, 80
thread, 65
turning tools, 78
webbing, 80

P
packing cubes, 19
pockets, 11, 88–92
portfolio bags, 18
pouches, 19
presser feet, 67–70
pressing tools, 73–74
purse frames, 87
purse hooks, 23

Q–R
quick references, 7–10
quilted bags, 8
rings, 51–53
rivets, 76
rucksacks, 12

S–T
saddle bags, 20
shaping and stabilizing, 82–85
shoulder bags, 20
side styles, 11
sling bags, 15
small bags, 10
snap fasteners, 77
straps, 11, 56, 92–94
structuring bags, 82–84
support materials, 38–39
tote bags, 21
tools. *See cutting tools; marking tools; pressing tools*

W–Z
waist bags, 21
wristlets, 14, 94
zippers, 58–63, 88–89

About the Author

JESSICA BARRERA is an author, designer, educator, and entrepreneur. She has been creatively sewing and crafting since the age of five. She studied entrepreneurship at the University of Wisconsin-Whitewater and now operates her own sewing pattern and supply company, Sallie Tomato. Her innovative designs and products aim to attract the next generations of sewing enthusiasts while appealing to current makers. Aside from running a business, she is a mom of two boys; loves coffee, home decorating, boutique shopping, traveling, yoga, and being outdoors; and is a fan of classic black-and-white movies. Jessica lives in Wisconsin with her family. Find her online at sallietomato.com and @sallietomatopatterns